In a world obsessed with fame and fortune, *Famous at Home* is exactly what families should aim for—being famous to the people who matter most. Josh and Christi wonderfully articulate how you can intentionally show up for your family and navigate the roadblocks that will inevitably appear. This is the perfect book for anyone wanting to become the best version of themselves not only for themselves, but for their family.

BOB GOFF, author of the *New York Times* bestsellers *Love Does*, *Everybody Always*, and *Dream Big*

I'm so thankful for friends like Josh and Christi and resources like *Famous at Home* as my wife and I navigate parenthood in such a busy season of life. We've become more motivated and intentional about learning how to be the best parents we can be for our three kids. This amazing book has helped us grow and educate ourselves around what it really means to be famous and what kind of fame is most important. This will be a book we read many times over the years as we continue to grow and navigate our most important responsibility and honor—being a parent.

TYLER HUBBARD, singer, songwriter, and musician

When Josh and Christi first mentioned the phrase "famous at home" a few years ago, I started clapping. It's such a perfectly simple, perfectly powerful way to think about the impact you can have inside your family. I knew the moment I heard their vision for this book that it was going to be a life-changing work. I'm so glad they're sharing this idea with more than just me over a cup of coffee in Nashville. This is a book that every parent could benefit from, and I couldn't be a bigger fan!

JON ACUFF, *New York Times* bestselli
Surprising Solution to Overthinking

The family is an "oven for growth" in which Mom, Dad, and their children all experience healthy ingredients such as attachment, structure, acceptance, and values. God's design is that each person then becomes well-adjusted, loving, and competent. So often, however, parents feel conflicted, overwhelmed, and disconnected from one another, and those stresses are replicated in their children. Josh and Christi Straub have provided a tremendous resource to help parents become the successful, close, and happy family they have always wanted. Using their own vulnerable narratives, examples of people they have worked with, the latest neuroscience and research, and biblical principles, they give the reader a right-now and practical guide to starting in a new and better way.

JOHN TOWNSEND, PhD, *New York Times* bestselling author of the Boundaries series, founder of the Townsend Institute for Leadership and Counseling and the Townsend Leadership Program

If you're like me, you've wasted so much time worrying over what other people think of you, only to realize none of it matters. This book is the antidote. I now want to be famous to only five people—my wife and four sons—because that's where fame matters and that's where my real mission is. This book is full of vulnerable moments and good stories, but most importantly, it will change you. Go read it. Quick.

JUSTIN WHITMEL EARLEY, business lawyer and author of *Habits of the Household: Practicing the Story of God in Everyday Family Rhythms*

We want to be famous in a lot of places—at work, in society, and in our towns. But Josh and Christi show us so clearly that if we want to have a true impact—in our work, society, and towns—it starts with being famous at home. This book is clear, wise, and full of truth.

> **JEFFERSON BETHKE**, *New York Times* bestselling author of *Jesus>Religion*

In a culture that prioritizes fame and success, our efforts to be recognized are often directed outward to the world rather than inward to our families. Then it is our families that get our tired, overwhelmed leftovers. In this book, Josh and Christi outline how to prioritize family. They offer reminders that those who too often get the least of us not only deserve but also bring out the best in us. I'm grateful for my friends Josh and Christi Straub—for their vulnerability, their passion for emotional health, and their commitment to bringing healing to families.

> **SISSY GOFF**, LPC, MHSP, director of child and adolescent counseling and bestselling author of *Raising Worry-Free Girls*

Famous at Home is not only timely but is also absolutely essential for anyone who desires to break the dysfunctional generational cycles they experienced growing up and ensure they are not repeated within their own family. Our friends Dr. Josh and Christi Straub not only provide a clear blueprint on how to do this but they teach it using their own lives. We highly recommend this book for those who are ready and serious about making their family a priority above all else.

> **JAMAL AND NATASHA MILLER**, CEO of Miller Media Group, Inc., and founders of The One University

In today's culture, it's too easy to find our value in what we do for a living. Josh and Christi remind us that there is something else that holds significantly more importance—our role in our families. As an actress, people may use the word *famous* to describe me, but I would much rather be famous at home to my four biggest, forever fans—my husband and three children. Take a dive into this purposeful book to refocus on leaving a meaningful legacy by putting your family center stage.

CANDACE CAMERON BURE, actress, producer, *New York Times* bestselling author

DR. JOSH AND CHRISTI STRAUB

FAMOUS AT HOME

7 Decisions to Put Your Family Center Stage in a World Competing for Your Time, Attention, and Identity

TYNDALE MOMENTUM®

A Tyndale nonfiction imprint

Visit Tyndale online at tyndale.com.

Visit Tyndale Momentum online at tyndalemomentum.com.

Visit Joshua and Christi Straub at famousathome.com.

Famous at Home: 7 Decisions to Put Your Family Center Stage in a World Competing for Your Time, Attention, and Identity

Designed by Sarah Susan Richardson

Edited by Christine M. Anderson

The authors are represented by Alive Literary Agency, www.aliveliterary.com.

Note: Names of all clients have been changed and some details of their stories modified to protect anonymity.

For information about special discounts for bulk purchases, please contact Tyndale House Publishers at csresponse@tyndale.com, or call 1-855-277-9400.

Library of Congress Cataloging-in-Publication Data

A catalog record for this book is available from the Library of Congress.

ISBN 978-1-4964-5486-7

Printed in the United States of America

28 27 26 25 24 23 22
7 6 5 4 3 2 1

To Landon, Kennedy, and Micah,

Wherever God leads you, trust him.

Whomever you serve, may it be from his love.

Whatever you do, may it be for his Kingdom.

You are and always will be famous at home.

CONTENTS

FOREWORD

Most Christian couples agree that family should be a priority in their lives. However, many lack a clear picture of what that looks like. Some think it means attending their kids' activities, such as recitals and athletic events. Others focus on giving their children experiences that create memories, such as elaborate birthday celebrations, exciting vacations, or adventurous world travel. Still other couples want to make sure their children have the best possible education, and they are often willing to sacrifice in order to provide it.

In some families, the marriage relationship is parked on a side street while the couple focuses on the well-being of the children. Other couples realize that keeping their marriage alive and vibrant is one of the best things they can do for their children. So they plan regular date nights, speak each other's love language, and do their best to process conflict in a healthy manner.

We all have our own ideas about what is most important in nurturing a healthy family, and we judge our success based on how well we do those things. We congratulate ourselves by saying, "I have only missed one of my son's ball games in the past two years." While this is commendable, all of us would probably agree that there is more to being a good parent than attending our children's events.

One of the saddest things I have ever heard was the lament of an adult son after the burial of his father. "I never knew my father," he said. "He worked out of town Monday through Friday, played golf on Saturday, and watched football on Sunday. He provided for us financially, but I never knew him." I walked away with tears in my eyes. My guess is that the father saw his role as financial provider and may have even congratulated himself for a job well done.

As Christians, our first allegiance is to God. Knowing him and serving him is our first priority. When we have this attitude, we pray, "Lord, show me how to invest my life in serving you by serving others. Where do I begin?" I believe God's answer is, "Begin with the people closest to you." If you are married, the person closest to you is your spouse; and if you have children, this includes them as well. Couples who love each other as Christ loves us begin by serving one another. That becomes our first priority in serving God. Then we seek together to follow the example of our heavenly Father in parenting our children.

In *Famous at Home*, Josh and Christi Straub share biblically based and practical ideas on how to put your family center stage by making it the focus of your service to God. When you prioritize serving one another in the home, you not only create an atmosphere in which your family can thrive, but you also equip your family to extend that attitude of service to others. I believe that one of the reasons the church has not made a greater impact on the world is that many Christians have never learned how to make service a way of life in the home. If you are eager to show up in meaningful ways for the loved ones under your roof and to make your family a launching pad for a life of ministry, *Famous at Home* points the way.

Gary Chapman, PhD
Author of The 5 Love Languages

AN INVITATION TO BE FAMOUS AT HOME

JOSH

It was September 2014 when I got the call. My dad's heart had failed. The left chamber was no longer able to pump blood into his organs. They, too, were shutting down.

In the three frantic hours that followed, with no flights available until the next day, Christi and I packed up all the belongings required for a six-week-old, a two-year-old, and two emotional adults to make a seventeen-hour, straight-through-the-night drive from Missouri to Hershey, Pennsylvania. With thirty minutes of sleep in a forty-two-hour span, we arrived in Hershey in time to see my dad coming out of surgery, where he had received a heart pump to do the work of his left chamber.

The next three weeks were difficult. Christi was living with in-laws while caring for a screaming two-month-old who didn't sleep and a needy two-year-old. I wasn't much help, as I spent most days driving an hour back and forth to the hospital and tried to work on the days in between.

Unbeknownst to us at the time, my dad would stay in the hospital another three months, needing another heart pump replacement by December. In mid-November, having returned home to

Missouri a few weeks prior, Christi and I flew out for a job interview I had for an executive position with a company on the other side of the country. It was the first time she had left our babies behind, and the trip was a disaster. On the day we arrived, Christi melted into tears during a meeting with the head of the human resources department. Just the impression I wanted to make, bringing an unsupportive and overwhelmed wife.

Here we were, in survival mode, our time pulled toward our high-maintenance babies and my dad's needs and facing a possible reprieve with a job that could give me a sense of identity I felt I was missing.

A month later, with dwindling finances, my dad still in the hospital fighting for his life, the looming prospect of moving across the country for a job, and a difficult four-month-old and two-year-old in tow, we inexplicably decided to drive twenty-one hours to spend Christmas with Christi's parents in Canada. Looking back, we have no idea what we were thinking.

To add chaos to chaos, two days before Christmas my dad surprised us all when he was released from the hospital. Now that we were just an eight-hour drive away at Christi's parents' house, all I could think about was my dad having a chance to hold his four-month-old granddaughter for the first time.

But Christi resisted.

Big time. With big-time tears.

I felt alone. Why couldn't she see my perspective?

But this wasn't one moment. This was a monthslong fade—one in which I had worked hard to keep all the plates spinning. And in my laser-focused efforts to fix everything and be everything for everyone, I became blind to what Christi had suffered.

In the previous five months, Christi had given birth, gotten little sleep, and been unable to breastfeed our daughter. Suffering from debilitating and chronic back pain, she had endured the seventeen-hour drive to Hershey, the three weeks living with in-laws, and the gut-wrenching trip across the country for a job opportunity that didn't pan out. Now, having driven twenty-one hours to Canada, I was demanding we drive another sixteen hours round trip back to Pennsylvania.

Convinced she was just being selfish, I packed up the kids and drove them, by myself, through an unexpected snow squall that had me petrified.

I made it, though. Saw my dad. And celebrated with him and the kids as best I could.

I thought I was putting my family center stage.

But upon my return, our marriage needed some work. Christi was bitter. In postpartum depression. On the bottom rung of life. She resented me, and I couldn't understand why. I felt like I was doing absolutely everything I could—getting up with the kids at night, cleaning the house, making a living, and honoring my parents. In my mind, I was crushing it.

In Christi's mind, nobody was crushing anything.

That was several years ago.

Today, we are each other's greatest teammates. Our gut instinct now is to fight *for* each other, not *against* each other. But Christi and I needed help to start functioning from our strengths. We weren't on the brink of divorce because it's not in our vocabulary, but we were emotionally and spiritually exhausted.

Not until we got honest about all that was stealing our time did we begin redeeming it for ourselves. Not until we saw what was robbing our attention did we turn it toward our family. And not until we were willing to look inward did we begin to see the unhealthy places we had put our identities. That's when we started fighting for each other. That's when we committed to making the decisions we needed to make moment by moment to find our way forward again—looking not merely to survive but to live fully alive, because our family was now center stage.

Putting Your Family Center Stage

Your family might not be as broken as we were at that time. On a family health scale of one to ten, with one being "hopeless" and ten being "crushing it," we were probably at about a three during that season. You may very well be on the crushing it end of the scale or at an eight and just looking for direction to sustain the health and growth your family already enjoys. Or perhaps your family is in the middle at a five, feeling like you're just going through the motions. You're not falling apart, but you're not fully connected, either, and you might feel stuck. Or maybe you're where we were, on the lower end of the scale, at a two, or on the brink of losing your family. You're really struggling and feeling hopeless.

Wherever you are right now, we wrote this book to help you move closer to the crushing it side of the scale, to help you become famous at home by putting your family center stage. That's not easy to do in a culture that competes for your time, attention, and identity. But when a career, a business endeavor, or any other role or activity takes center stage, it's all too easy for your family to get your leftovers instead of your best.

The pull toward work or any other endeavor that affirms our identity often provides a dopamine bump in our brain that being at home with our loved ones does not. Crushing it on our "stage" for superiors, stakeholders, or followers provides a much higher level of instant gratification than an oft-interrupted game of Chutes and Ladders in which our opponent struggles to know which way is up and which is down. Our ego also knows the difference between the accolades of our coworkers, fans, followers, or customers and the appreciation (insert sarcasm) we receive at home.

Many of us put more effort into becoming famous on stages outside the home because that's where we find our identity and significance. Your stage could be on social media, in a boardroom, on a sports field, in a hospital, on the battlefield, in a government building, on a farm, in an arena, or in any other role or activity to which you attach your sense of significance. But putting a career or any other source of identity center stage can wreak havoc on the relationships with the ones you love the most.

For some, their stage is the home. Think of the stay-at-home parent on the front lines raising kids and supporting the oftentimes more public or, in the eyes of the world, "more important" stage of his or her spouse. Cooking meals for, picking up after, and chauffeuring tantrum-throwing, nitpicking, and unappreciative kids all day leaves even the most intentional stay-at-home parent feeling unseen and insignificant.

As a marriage and leadership coach to high-capacity leaders and organizations, I see firsthand the toll that putting work center stage takes on the home. I've seen it in military officers, Forbes 500 executives, musicians, pastors, professional athletes, and husband/wife entrepreneurs—no matter the stage, the ache for deeper family connection is the same.

Christi and I often hear phrases like these:

- "I lead hundreds at work but feel like I can't lead anyone in my own home."
- "My spouse and I have sadly become roommates."
- "I feel like all I get is his/her leftovers."
- "I feel like all I have to give is what's left over."
- "I feel unappreciated at home."

No one wakes up one day and decides, "I'm going to ruin my marriage, neglect my kids, and cause mistrust in my family." Yet our busyness and personal pursuits—our time and attention pulled in other places—can create a slow fade that leads toward just that. The problem for each of us is that the lure toward the immediate gratification of achievement and success outside the home can wreak long-term havoc inside the home.

The promise of *Famous at Home* is that you really can show up in intentional and meaningful ways for your biggest fans—the loved ones under your roof. You can have healthy personal rhythms that enable you to show up as the best version of you for your family. You can have a rock-solid marriage—one in which you and your spouse fight *for* rather than *against* one another. And you can have a mission for your family, a purpose that enables you and your kids to feel part of something so much bigger than yourselves alone.

This is what can happen when you put your family center stage.

How to Read *Famous at Home*

Famous at Home includes the practical and life-changing coaching strategies we use with our clients, but we also live this stuff ourselves. We never ask anybody to do something we're not willing to do. As you read and work through the book, you'll be invited into the ups and downs of our own story. You'll also meet families we've had the privilege of coaching through our organization, Famous at Home. Every story is real, though the names and details have been altered to protect the families' privacy.

You may find it helpful to have a journal or notebook with you as you read. In addition to writing down notes and personal insights along the way, you'll need a place to write your responses to coaching exercises. As an option, we've also created downloadable worksheets you can use to complete the coaching exercises. Access the Famous at Home worksheets at www.famousathome.com/book.

Famous at Home is organized in three parts. In part 1, "What It Means to Be Famous," we explore who was famous for you and why it matters. We'll also consider what you might be chasing as a source of identity and significance. Where you place your identity often speaks into the struggles you have as a family. It can also impact your willingness, or unwillingness, to make the decisions necessary to be famous at home.

In part 2, "An Overnight Success a Decade in the Making," we focus on the daily perseverance required to become famous at home. Just as there are famous musicians who put in years of hard work before becoming a seeming overnight success, there is hard work to be done to put your family center stage. We'll walk you through the deeper work you can do in your emotional and spiritual life to build a foundation for genuinely putting your family center stage over the long haul.

In part 3, "Seven Decisions to Put Your Family Center Stage," we walk you step-by-step through a process to help you discover and live out your family's purpose in everyday, doable ways. When you apply the Seven Decisions to put your family center stage, you'll learn how to better care for yourself so you can show up for your family. We'll help you develop an emotional vocabulary to better understand the inner worlds of your loved ones, as well as daily practices you can use to connect with your spouse and kids at a heart level. As you work through various coaching exercises, you'll establish your family rhythms, family values, and a family mission that gives meaning and direction to your family purpose.

No matter where you currently are on the family health scale, whether on the low end of hopeless or the high end of crushing it, we believe the relationship you have with your spouse and kids can be filled with connection, adventure, and purpose. Even if you don't have much hope for that right now, let us hold that hope for you. You really can leave a legacy for your kids that will echo throughout the generations. And the good news is this: *It's never too late to get started.*

We have seen dire circumstances turn into beautiful marriage stories. We have seen fractured parent/child relationships fully restored. We have seen families on the verge of falling apart rebuild such life-giving relationships that they became a source of hope for other families. All because one person—yes, it takes just one person—was willing to make some new decisions. Decisions that didn't require a lot of time, but that shifted the atmosphere of the home—from exhaustion to rest, from resentment to forgiveness, from distrust to trust. We can't wait for you to read the stories of how this happens and how it can work for your family as well.

This is your invitation. Let's be famous at home.

★

PART I

WHAT IT MEANS TO BE FAMOUS

JOSH

Following dinner at the home of friends, our family arrived home about an hour and a half past our kids' bedtime. When I walked in to pray with our son Landon, he was standing beside his bed looking out of sorts.

"Dad, I knew I was going to do that," he said, disheartened. In what felt like slow motion, I watched as his bottom lip started to quiver and his eyes filled with tears.

"Buddy, what's going on?" I asked, sitting on the edge of his bed as I pulled him in close.

"I left my rubber band at Braxton's house."

"A rubber band? I can buy you a whole bag of rubber bands," I said, going into fix-it mode.

Sobbing, he continued. "No, Dad, this was my spec-spec-special rubber band. I wasn't even going to take it with me, but I did anyway, and now I forgot it. I know right where I put it, too."

I had a decision to make as a dad. Was he overtired? Sure he was. Was he overvaluing a rubber band? In my mind, yes. But did this mean something to him? You bet it did.

I grabbed my phone and texted Braxton's dad as Landon watched. Still not grasping the magnitude of the moment, I tucked Landon into bed, prayed with him, and kissed him goodnight.

As I went to brush my teeth, I got a text. The rubber band was in safe hands. I'd be picking it up off our friends' front porch in the morning.

I can't believe I'm picking up a rubber band, I kept thinking.

I walked back to Landon's room and told him the good news.

"Dad," he said, sitting up in bed, "you're the best! Thank you so much for helping me get it back."

I was leveled by the importance of the moment. I had no idea how much time he spent with that rubber band. He used it for

Lego builds, racetracks, and other engineering contraptions. This rubber band was essential to so many projects it had its own place on his nightstand—and in his heart.

Looking back, I'm glad I handled it the way I did. Had I made the moment about me, playing the hero by buying a whole bag of new rubber bands, or playing into my parental fear by belittling the rubber band as something not worth crying about, or playing into Landon's carelessness for taking something he knew he'd lose to a friend's house, I would have missed the sweet experience of his gratitude and mile-wide smile.

You might still be thinking, *It was a rubber band. The kid was tired. You're making something out of nothing.* I might be. But I don't want to risk the consequences of accumulated failed opportunities to enter my child's world because I make the moment about me. Instead, I want to make the choices that will make me famous to my kids.

That's why part 1, "What It Means to be Famous," takes you back to who was famous for you and why it matters. So often, we are unable to show up in these ordinary but meaningful "rubber band" moments with our loved ones because somewhere on our journey we left behind our own inner child. And in a renewed search for significance, we give our time, attention, and identity over to anything that will fill the emotional void, bolster our ego, and heal our pain—a chase that can make us famous, but perhaps not in the way we imagined.

Capturing those sweet experiences of gratitude and mile-wide smiles from your biggest fans often requires rediscovering your own mile-wide smile. Let's go figure out what's stealing it and what it really means for you to be famous.

1

BEING FAMOUS

Who Showed Up for You?

JOSH

The house was situated right next to a country road in rural central Pennsylvania, but it wasn't one of those lonely country roads that winds slowly through the hills. No, it was a 45 mph bypass for the 55 mph main drag from one town to the next.

The house also sat smack in the middle of a concrete block manufacturer. Across the road was a lot filled with block trucks, gas tanks, and maintenance garages. Flying dust was common as trucks came and went, taking the next round of blocks to a job site, perhaps to build the basement walls of someone's new home.

The inventory lived on the same side of the road as the house. Stacks of cinder blocks, massive bins of sand, stones of all shapes and sizes, and topsoil were piled right against the back and side yards of the house—a child's playground dreams come true!

My sister and I were the beneficiaries because our grandmother lived in this house. Mispronouncing "grandma" when I was a little boy was one of the best mistakes of my life, as my grandma became affectionately known as "Me-maw" to everyone around her. And affection is what I felt in her presence. Deep feelings of joy, connection, and safety. Not to mention the sensory comforts that seemed to saturate my soul every time I walked through her door.

The taste of ham, sweet potatoes, and the fixings of fresh homemade meals every holiday.

The smell of freshly cut grass and the sight of the poplar leaves that changed color with each season.

The sounds of laughter every Sunday afternoon as we played games in that old house.

The feel of glue, pipe cleaners, and beads while making homemade Christmas ornaments.

Loving intentionality motivated everything Me-maw did. And all of it gave me a much-needed sense of stability and safety in the years following my parents' divorce when I was ten years old.

To the outside world, Me-maw wasn't known. But to me, nobody was more famous.

If I had a bad week at school and needed to smile again, I knew I'd be going to Me-maw's house that weekend. When there was turmoil in the family, I went to see Me-maw. No matter what life threw at me, Me-maw was my stability. Her consistent presence kept me safe, gave me hope, and allowed me to be me.

Today, if you were to walk through the cemetery to the plot where Ruth Straub is buried, you would see one word under her name on the headstone: "Me-Maw." There's no question what made her famous.

We trusted her to show up.

Who Is Famous to You?

Growing up, who was your Me-maw? Who allowed you to be you? When you felt afraid, who was the calming presence that helped you reenter the world with confidence? Whom did you run to for hope when it seemed like everyone else had let you down? Who put a smile on your face when you felt sad? Did your parents provide this sense of safety for you? Or was it another family member, such as an aunt or uncle or a grandparent? Was it a coach, a close family friend, a foster parent?

What did your Me-maw's house look like? Smell like? Taste like? Sound like? Feel like? Was it your own home? The home of a friend? A school, a rec center, or a youth camp? Give yourself the gift of a few minutes to go back in time and recall that person and that place in your mind's eye.

At Famous at Home, we do an exercise similar to this at the start of a yearlong coaching program called the Leader's Heart Cohort. This cohort is like a business mastermind mentoring group, except we focus on the leader's inner life more than the leader's professional life. At the first meeting, we ask participants to introduce themselves to the group using the words of someone—living or deceased—who believes or believed in them.

I love watching the participants' faces during this exercise. Some light up thinking of the person who loved them dearly. Others smile hesitantly, wanting to believe that the good things coming out of their mouths hold true, but not yet believing those words themselves.

Every now and again, some participants have a difficult time thinking of anyone who believed in them. At that point, we ask if a pet loved or championed them. If not, we move to a moment in their lives in which a coach, teacher, parent, pastor, or friend encouraged or stood up for them. Or we simply invite them to "tell us about a time when you felt loved."

We all deserve to be loved. To have someone who shows up for us. The Bible says, "Such love has no fear, because perfect love expels all fear" (1 John 4:18). When I was a child, Me-maw's love calmed my fears. Me-maw's house was an emotional safe haven.

Being famous at home is about showing up in love for our spouse and kids. And we show up best when we do so from a place of feeling truly loved ourselves.

What It Means to Be Famous

In twenty-first-century America, fame often comes by way of an extraordinary talent or skill, such as acting, dancing, singing, or athletics. For the most part, we tend to celebrate people who entertain us. That includes social media celebrities and influencers. But the relationship we have with famous people is a one-way street—we know who they are, but they have no idea who *we* are. They don't show up for us when we feel sad. They don't celebrate our parenting wins. They don't connect with us when we need a listening ear.

We can't trust them to show up. Nor should we.

Yet, clinging to the picture-perfect worlds of famous people is perhaps one reason why teenage and young adult loneliness, depression, anxiety, and suicide continue to rise, while happiness, life satisfaction, and flourishing decline. Kids who have grown up following famous online influencers desire the glamorous life these celebrities appear to live, but they lack the basic relational skills required to navigate even an ordinary life well. They don't know how to ask for help or have a heartfelt human connection with anyone willing to enter their pain or simply hold their hand through it.[1] Screen time does not and cannot fulfill the deepest relational longings of our hearts.

Recall again the one person who showed up for you when you were a child, even if it was in a single moment. In showing up, they gave you a visceral taste of heaven on earth. Love to calm your soul. Trust to settle your mind. Permission to be yourself.

The beloved disciple John described the source of such experiences of feeling loved when he wrote, "We love each other because [God] loved us first" (1 John 4:19). How well we step into the shoes of another person's world and truly love them for who they are without making it about us flows from feeling loved by God. We tap into that feeling when we recall how someone showed up for us when we were a child. Experiencing the love of a trusted adult in childhood is foundational for how well we show up for others when we become adults.

Jesus drew on this transformational experience of divine love when he addressed his disciples shortly before his arrest and crucifixion: "Dear children, I will be with you only a little longer" (John 13:33). At first glance, it might seem condescending to address other adults as children. But Jesus used this affectionate address for his disciples only once in the Gospels,[2] and understanding the context in which he used it makes it even more meaningful. The Greek word that translates to "Dear children" is *teknion*. It is a term that conveys deep affection. Jesus used it to express his heartfelt tenderness toward his disciples right before he gave them a new commandment: "Just as I have loved you, you should love each other" (John 13:34). Did you catch the connection? Before commanding them to love, he wanted them to know they were loved by him.

The apostle Paul built on this teaching when he wrote, "I pray that you, being rooted and established in love, may . . . *know* [Christ's] love that surpasses *knowledge*—that you may be filled to the measure of all the fullness of God" (Ephesians 3:17-19,

NIV, emphasis added). Notice how Paul used wordplay to make a distinction between two kinds of knowing. To have "knowledge" (the Greek word *gnosis*) is to know about God; but "to know" (the Greek word *ginosko*) "indicates a relation between the person 'knowing' and the object known."[3] In other words, we can know about God, but Paul wants us to experience—to "be aware (of), feel . . . be sure, [and] understand"—God's love, because it fills us with "all of the fullness of God."[4]

When we experience this kind of love from God, it frees us from the spirit of judgment, shame, and condemnation. We become free to be ourselves and to show up for others because we trust God to show up for us.

We can show up selflessly for our spouse because God first loved us.

We can love our kids as Jesus loves us because we, too, are his children.

We can participate in divine love and show up for others filled with the fullness of God.

That's because God created human relationships to function in much the same way, giving us a taste of heaven on earth as we experience his love through others who show up for us.

Though my relationship with Me-maw when I was growing up was filled with loving experiences, there were other relatives with whom I had no experiences—I merely knew about them. It was Me-maw's showing up that rooted and established me in love, a love that helped me to become the husband and dad I am today. Now I get to pass on the fullness of her love by loving my kids the way she loved me.

Though you may not always get it right in the moment, your ongoing presence and commitment to showing up in the lives of your spouse and kids instills in them the fullness of your love.

When you're famous to the world, you're renowned and celebrated for a talent or skill. But when you're famous at home, you're renowned and celebrated for showing up in the one place that matters most.

Twenty Years from Now

I'll never forget teaching our daughter, Kennedy, to ride her bike without training wheels. I did wind sprints up and down our road, holding the bike loosely enough to help her learn but tightly enough that she wouldn't fall. I encouraged her. I picked her up when she scraped her ankle on the pedal. I told her she had what it took to ride on two wheels. She just needed me to believe in her more than she believed in herself.

Two nights later, Christi and I watched our daughter ride her bicycle around the cul-de-sac without training wheels like a pro. I stood on the sidewalk cheering like a raving lunatic, with a high probability of embarrassing Kennedy had others been watching but an even higher probability of giving her a taste of the raving love our Father in heaven has for us.

It is the accumulation of moments like this one, of showing up every day, that help our children *know* they are loved.

With this in mind, fast-forward twenty years from now. What do you hope your grown child might say if a friend were to ask, "Who showed up for you when you were a kid?" What moments do you hope your adult child will remember?

Though Kennedy might not remember me cheering like a lunatic the night she learned to ride a bike, I hope she grows up feeling loved and celebrated in all of her "bike riding" moments. In her mind's eye, I hope she always sees me jumping up and down for her achievements, hears my voice cheering her on, and feels my embrace in her failures as well as her successes. And I hope all of it becomes the fuel that enables her to be brave in every circumstance she encounters as an adult.

Can you show up for your kids in absolutely every moment? Probably not. But you can show up, and the ordinary moments add up. You can tuck your kids into bed each night. You can watch a ball game, a dance recital, or a gymnastics meet. You can hold your kids in their distress, laugh with them at the dinner table, or teach them something you know. No act of showing up is ever wasted.

All of it is fuel.

All of it is "fame."

2

ALMOST FAMOUS

What Are You Chasing?

CHRISTI

One of the most iconic and storied movies of the past few years is *The Greatest Showman*, a film based on the life of famed circus creator P. T. Barnum. The soundtrack alone is epic. Our family, led by the kids, unashamedly recreates scenes from the movie with dance parties in our house. Stage lights. Microphones. Karaoke machines. The ringmaster's hat. We do it right.

Though the music is one of the best soundtracks of all time, the story is equally compelling.

Most of us can relate to what I call the "chase" of P. T. Barnum.

A man who comes from poverty, Barnum wins the heart of his childhood sweetheart, a young woman raised in wealth and the social status that comes with it. And even though she never asks for it, Barnum vows to give her the life her parents provided her growing up.

One of the most beautiful images of lowly beginnings happens early in their marriage, up on the rooftop of their humble apartment building. The family now has two little girls, and their laughter fills the night sky as their dancing silhouettes move effortlessly between clotheslines hung with sheets. That rooftop moment captures a scene we all long for. Everyone together. Present in the moment. Full of joy.

Except for P. T. Barnum himself. Deep within, he remains unsettled, his face showing it all. Longing to soak in the pure joy of the moment but driven to prove he has what it takes to give his family a life of grandeur, Barnum starts chasing—success, fame, and fortune.

Maybe you can relate. Perhaps you know the tension of being in one of these rooftop moments, watching your kids play without a care in the world. And all the while, you're trying to settle the flying monkeys in your mind, trying not to ruin the purity of the moment, trying to soak in the joyous laughter.

For a second, such rooftop moments might make us question the chase. But the unsettledness within keeps us on the move. We reason that life could be better than it is now if only we had whatever it is we're chasing.

For Barnum, that meant chasing larger crowds. Increased notoriety. Outrageous acts. More money. But all such stories end in familiar ways, and Barnum's was no different. His chase nearly cost him everything, including the very thing he chased it all for in the first place—his family.

Like Barnum, we all begin our chase with sincere intentions. But as the drive to prove our worth emerges, the dopamine rush of more accolades, bigger fanfare, better social status, more money, or feelings of significance keeps us chasing. And what we lose while chasing what we think we need is rarely, if ever, worth it.

How Christi's Chase Began

My chase started in obscurity.

I was standing in the kitchen of our little ranch home in Branson, Missouri, with our six-month-old firstborn son, Landon. I was grateful to stay home with him, but motherhood wasn't coming as instinctively as I thought it should. Other mothers around me seemed to fall into the role quite naturally, making it look easy. My experience was anything but, though I didn't know it was okay to say so.

I was wearing my newly acquired mom uniform—no makeup, hair in a ponytail, baggy T-shirt from Josh's closet, college volleyball sweatpants—all of it spackled in banana and puréed sweet potato. While I was teaching our sweet boy to eat solid foods, Josh waltzed into the house wafting in the aroma of some delicious latte. I could only assume it came from one of those adorable coffee shops with moody, relaxing background music—the perfect environment for working and allowing you to hear your own thoughts. I, on the other hand, had spent the day with crying as my background music and longed to talk to someone who could tie their shoes.

As Josh sauntered in, calm and relaxed, he started to talk about his day, whom he met with, and all the exciting projects he had going on. I was quite the juxtaposition—frazzled, anxious, unkempt, and achingly alone. As I stood there in all my banana-and-sweet-potato-spackled glory, something within me burst, and tears, oh so many tears, started to flow.

The only words I could find in that moment were, "Why do you never ask me about me? It's always about you. You never ask about what's on my heart."

My feelings spewed out as arrows toward Josh.

Until that moment, I hadn't known how hidden I felt.

Though I didn't have the words at the time, I felt alone, invisible, and left behind. Caught off guard by this outburst of insecurity and exhaustion, Josh had nothing to say in response. My outburst had made him feel like a failure and overwhelmed him. He just pulled me in and held me as my tears flowed.

I hadn't intended to cast all the blame on him, but that's often how we react when we're drowning—we try to scramble on top of someone else and end up pushing them down farther than us. I wasn't okay, and I needed him to feel how horrible it felt, so I shot my arrows in his direction. This new life of parenting was not what I'd expected. It was taking all I had to give and more. If I was drowning and Josh was thriving, I reasoned that my predicament had to be his fault.

It's been several years since that day in the kitchen, and while many things have changed for the better, I still struggle with the chase for significance. Though I work for Famous at Home as cofounder and vice president, most of what I do is behind the scenes. In fact, virtually every other title I carry includes the word "home."

Homemaker.

Homeschool teacher.

Stay-at-home mom (for the most part).

If we were to sit down for coffee and you asked me what I struggle with now, I'd tell you it's still the hiddenness. I feel invisible. Unimportant. At times, lonely.

I am home. I live and work and school from home. I'm with my children most of the hours in a week. I'm in their lives and striving to know their hearts. Although I'm far from perfect, I know I am truly giving my all. Yet, like the flying monkeys that vie for attention in pure moments of family laughter, the question jumping around my mind is not, "Is what I'm doing significant?" because I know it is. The aching question is, "Am *I* significant?"

For my children's sake, I know deep down the work of parenting is worth it. But if I'm really honest, it doesn't make *me* feel significant.

I'm not ashamed to admit that. In fact, it's a relief to say it aloud. I want to be seen and respected. Society doesn't recognize the work stay-at-home parents do to make a home, to shape a young life, or to mold a little heart. We don't get an awards show, golden trophies, or performance evaluations to reassure us we're seen and making a difference.

On the contrary, society seems to denigrate the work done within the walls of a home, considering it of far lesser significance than work done outside the home. And therein lies the rub, as Shakespeare said. If you are a parent who works at home, you're stuck between a rock and a hard place.

I know I'm privileged to stay at home with my kids. Working moms may envy my position. But privately, I often envy theirs. In the day-to-day of parenting, we all long for more significance. Moms working outside the home long to feel more significant inside the home. Moms inside the home long to feel more significant to anyone outside who can tie a shoe.

Stuck between so many roles and often feeling ashamed to admit our pain, we shoot emotional arrows at our spouse. And we keep chasing.

How Josh's Chase Began

JOSH

Monday, July 9, 1990.

A hot summer Pennsylvania day.

The perfect weather for a ten-year-old boy to play with his friends at the creek, ride a bike, and swim. But since we'd been at the beach the weekend before on a family vacation, sleeping in felt right.

At 6:04 a.m., my life changed.

I remember hearing someone crying as I glanced at the clock and then saw a blurry vision of my mom walking into my bedroom with my little sister close behind her.

As I sat up in bed, my mom sat down.

"Josh," she said, "I'm moving out today. Do you want to go with me or stay here with your dad?"

How does a ten-year-old answer that question?

"What's Jenna doing?" I asked.

"Going with me," Mom answered.

I chose to stay with my dad.

Sort of.

Fast-forward twenty-eight years to when, now as a husband and dad myself, I hit a wall—a figurative one to be sure, though I'm convinced a cement wall would have been more forgiving. Paralyzing fear unlike anything I had ever experienced woke me up to a pattern in my life, a pattern that went back to those early years of parenting that Christi just wrote about.

With accumulated stress came accumulated fear. Now when Christi's arrows came at me, I had nothing left to give. Instead of reaching out to hug her like I did in the kitchen years earlier, I got defensive—every emotion convincing me I had to defend my honor. But time and again, even with my guard up, I'd put my head down and do what I had to do to ensure the house was in order. I was up at night with the kids. Then I'd get up the next morning, go to work, come home, take over with the kids, do bath time, go to bed for a while, and wake up with the kids once again through the night.

Repeat.

Day after day.

In my mind, I was crushing it.

Whenever Christi felt overwhelmed or accused me of not pursuing her heart, I'd once again defend my honor, ask where in the world she expected me to give more (which was how I played the victim), and then make necessary adjustments to hold everyone together, albeit temporarily.

And that right there is what I didn't realize until it finally caught up with me in the form of paralyzing fear. My chase was all about holding everyone together, which meant I, too, had to have it all together.

But the hold-it-all-together bandages I kept putting on our infected relational wounds were no longer enough. In the moments when I felt as if I couldn't do it anymore on my own, I crashed. Each crash worse than the one before it. That was the cycle. I put my head down, worked hard, then crashed. Looking back into my story, I couldn't figure out why I hadn't experienced fear and burnout like this when I was single.

Once the dust settled following my parents' divorce, I chose to go back and forth—one week at my mom's house, one week at my dad's house. I didn't want anybody to feel left out. For decades, I thought I was protecting everyone else.

I had done some therapy over the years to work through the emotional fallout from my parents' divorce, and in my twenties, my mom's porch swing became a sacred place of healing for the two of us as we reconciled parts of our broken past together. Today, our relationship couldn't be stronger.

But I had never paid much attention to the relationship with my dad. He'd always been there. In fact, I could count on one hand the number of my wrestling matches he'd missed when I was growing up—he was always in the stands. In my mind, once I healed the relationship with my mom, I was set.

That is, until I went to an intensive therapeutic retreat

comprised of six days in group therapy with complete strangers who became a second family. In my group, I was asked to do a family sculpture. My amazing therapist, Mary, asked me to reenact July 9, 1990, this time with others playing my family members and someone else stepping in for "little Josh." Becoming the director of my childhood movie, I recounted the moments of that day and watched as other people brought my story to life.

Having reconciled many parts of that day in previous therapy, I was somewhat stoic as I watched the events unfold before me. Then, we went to the driveway.

The driveway scene!

How had I blocked the entirety of the driveway scene out of my awareness all these years? The tears began to flow.

My dad had been at work the day my mom moved her belongings out of the house. Though the conversation remains foggy, I hold a vivid "mind picture" of the four of us standing in the driveway after my dad arrived home, all of us in tears, when one of my friends went riding by on her bicycle, a spectator to our crumbling family unit.

Seeing my dad in tears, I assured him I was staying with him. Though I'm certain I never voiced it then, I had a strong visceral reaction that came to life during my childhood movie, one in which I essentially relayed the message, "Dad, I will take care of you. I got this."

At ten years old, I assumed the role of fixer in the family, the one who tried to hold everyone together. Unfortunately, nobody knew how to tell that ten-year-old boy that such a responsibility wasn't his to carry.

In group therapy, my now good friend Tyler played the role of little Josh. I watched as our therapist piled pillows onto his outstretched arms, one after the other, each pillow representing a responsibility I had carried. Then Mary asked me to switch places with Tyler, and I began holding the pillows. I hadn't thought pillows would require a lot of strength to hold up—until they were stacked so high I could barely balance them and my arms began to ache from holding the same position for what felt like hours. At first, I rested my arms on my legs. But then Tyler piped up, "Dude, you can't do that. You need to hold those things like I did."

He was right. I was trying to cheat because it was all too heavy.

Tears flowed again, just as they had in the driveway that hot summer day in 1990. Holding those pillows, I felt the weight of all the responsibilities for other people I had no business carrying.

Looking back, it began to make sense to me. When Christi spiraled downward in those early years of parenting, I did all I could to hold everyone together. In addition to carrying Christi and the kids, I took on responsibility for my dad, who was sick with congestive heart failure. I also felt responsible in many ways for the emotional well-being of my stepmom, mom, stepdad, and Christi's concerned family. Not to mention the families and leaders I coached in the context of my work responsibilities. Whenever the pillows of life began to stack up, each one proving I didn't have it all together, I'd crash under the weight of it all. And in the process of carrying that heavy load, ten-year-old Josh was long forgotten.

The Things We Chase

CHRISTI

Whether you're a stay-at-home or working parent, a businessman like P. T. Barnum, an entrepreneur, mompreneur, celebrity, or laborer, you know that as fellow sojourning humans, we all search for significance. We want to know our worth, and we want to know that the mark we leave on the world matters.

But when these deep longings of the heart go unmet, we chase. We look to comfort our feelings of insignificance, overwhelm, insecurity, hiddenness, and loneliness by chasing their opposite—feelings of significance, rest, security, renown, and love. Too often, though, as Johnny Lee famously sang, we have a knack for "looking for love in all the wrong places."

Like P. T. Barnum looking for his worth in wealth and renown, or me screaming for significance by shooting arrows at my husband, or Josh seeking security in making sure everyone around him was okay, we all, in our own way, employ faulty strategies for rediscovering or shoring up our worth. However, in doing so, we turn to counterfeits that pull us further away from those we love.

Chasing these seemingly important, temporarily fulfilling, but ultimately vain pursuits of fame outside of the home can lead to a loveless marriage, disconnected family, divorce, scandalous affair, or deep regret later in life. King Solomon wrote about this when he said, "All people spend their lives scratching for food, but they never seem to have enough" (Ecclesiastes 6:7). Put another way, "We work to feed our appetites; meanwhile our souls go hungry" (Ecclesiastes 6:7, MSG). And to keep us chasing, our spiritual adversary uses the ordinary stuff of everyday life against us—long hours, travel, finances, kids, activities, even our past—so that we'll drop our guard with our family.

No wonder we are so easily distracted during our rooftop moments, wishing we could be more present, more connected with our loved ones, but focused on the chase instead. The more we numb our uncomfortable emotions with counterfeit attempts at feeling good about ourselves, the more we numb our positive emotions as well, robbing us of our ability to be fully present in the moment.

That's why the first step toward freedom and peace of mind in those rooftop moments is to recognize and name the underlying motivation behind the things you chase:

Financial security.

Significance.

Feeling valued.

Being invited.

A sense of control.

Proving your worth.

Keeping everyone happy.

Fear of missing out.

(Fill in your underlying motivation here.)

One of the ways to identify your underlying motivation is to write down what most occupies your mind in those figurative, or perhaps literal, rooftop moments with your family. Simply naming your motivation gives you some measure of power over it. But naming it takes courage, vulnerability, and the safety of people who love you enough to listen.

As a married couple who also work together, our insecurities often feed on one another, which only makes things worse when we're both not doing well. Recently, in one thirty-second span, I snapped at the kids, cut off Josh as he was telling me a story, and lost my temper when my shirt got caught on the drying rack in the kitchen.

Josh bravely stepped into the moment. "Christi, what's going on?"

The truth was that I had never felt more overwhelmed as a wife, mom, and business owner all at once.

Later that night, after we had time to cool off, Josh and I sat down together to talk through what each of us were chasing. Feeling overwhelmed and fearful, Josh had been withdrawing, chasing to protect what he believed others thought of him. I was losing my temper, and a major part of that was my chase for control as I watched Josh withdraw. We both were at fault, and we both had to name the motivations underlying our crazy behaviors.

Once we were able to be vulnerable about our insecurities and what was happening, we spent time in prayer together, repenting of our actions and surrendering our chasing to God. Not until we named what we were chasing—with one another and then with God—were we calm enough to show up in a more loving way for one another and for our kids.

Walking this journey together is a wild, sometimes heated, but always beautiful ride, and we wouldn't trade it for anything. For us, going deep is living life to the full. If your spouse isn't ready to go there or you don't yet feel safe talking to him or her about your "chase," writing your story in a journal or asking a good friend to journey with you is a great way to get started.

Josh and I continue to walk this decades-long journey of vulnerability because, for us, the rewards—now and in the future—are worth it. I don't want to be almost famous to my kids, a one-hit wonder whose kids spent more time begging me to get off my phone than playing with me.

Your real legacy as a parent happens when you drop the counterfeit chase to prove your worth and choose to chase with courage those seemingly obscure rooftop moments day after day. Everyone together. Present in the moment. Full of joy.

3

YOUR BIGGEST FANS

What Do Your Followers Really See?

CHRISTI

When I found out we were pregnant with Kennedy, our second child and first daughter, I was initially elated; but then an odd sense of sadness set in. I realized my days with just our firstborn were numbered. Where had the time with Landon gone? I felt the pace of life picking up. The baby days were a blur. I mourned all the losses I felt.

Why hadn't I held him longer? Why hadn't I watched him sleep more, enjoying the gentle and beautiful rhythm of his little chest rising and falling? Why hadn't I taken more time to notice his perfectly formed little hands curl around mine as we read books? Why hadn't I lavished my attention on the way his little eyelashes flutter with excitement over blowing bubbles?

The moments were slipping by, out from under me, while I was consumed by to-do lists, chasing things that felt urgent, and distracted by devices.

I was missing out on life.

What could be so important that I was willing to exchange moments with this precious, fully alive little boy to gaze at a cold, unfeeling screen? Obviously, it wasn't the screen. Something deeper was behind it.

If you had asked me then who I was trying to impress with my life, I'd have given you the Sunday school answer—God, my husband, and my kids. But good intentions are not synonymous with intentionality. Intentionality is the *reality* of the good we intend to do; it is the visible evidence of our invisible good intentions.

When it comes to your family, you no doubt have good intentions. But if you were to look at your calendar, checkbook, and screen time over the past six months, would the evidence of intentionality be proof of your good intentions? Those three things are the acid tests for me. Because how I spend my time, money, and mental energy—especially on social media—is a much better indicator of my priorities than my good intentions.

Ask yourself, "Based on my calendar, checkbook, and screen time, who am I trying to impress? Whom do I hope to win over? Who gets the best of who I am?"

Where am I spending my time?

Who has my attention?

To what am I attaching my identity?

I'll just let these questions hang there for a minute. I don't think they're ones we can answer quickly or honestly until we dig a bit deeper.

The Bottom Rung of Life

When Josh and I were first married, my dream was to have children and be involved in marriage and family ministry. Filled with naiveté, I had no idea what those things would require of me.

I write these words on the eve of my daughter's fifth birthday. This very night five years ago, I went to sleep very pregnant, uncomfortable, and achy, with no idea it would be the last night of my former life. The next day, I birthed a beautiful baby girl with dark brown hair, blue eyes, and lungs full of power. That was the day my life changed.

Her older brother, Landon, a feisty almost-two-year-old at the time, had already flipped our world upside down, but it was this girl who was about to break me apart. Kennedy Rae, my beautiful baby girl, was born healthy and whole, a mother's dream, I realize.

But she cried.

A lot.

Kennedy, our precious gift, came home and spent the next few weeks screaming. Like we dropped her on the floor kind of screaming. I became known around our community as "the woman with the baby with the worst cry I've ever heard." She slept in twenty-four- to forty-three-minute increments through the night. I know because we timed it. And then, just as Josh figured out a way to dance her back to sleep and ever so delicately transition her into the crib, she'd wake up screaming again.

We visited doctors, lactation specialists, chiropractors, and the like. Every Tom, Dick, and Susy had advice or an opinion on why she didn't sleep and screamed so much, but none of it helped, and nothing made a difference. This began my slow descent toward what I not so affectionately refer to as the "bottom rung of life."

I look back now and know I was struggling with depression, anxiety, adrenal fatigue, and post-traumatic stress reactions. But at the time, I pressed on, grateful for my daughter's life while struggling to bond with her.

One morning, Josh found me curled up and sobbing on the

bathroom floor. I was Kennedy's mother, but there was nothing I could do to get her to sleep or stop crying.

To add insult to injury, my back had been a constant problem since my college volleyball days. After Kennedy was born, it got worse. I couldn't lower her into or lift her out of her crib. I couldn't sit or stand for long periods of time. I couldn't walk around the block. When Kennedy was six months old, I threw my back out during a diaper change and couldn't walk for three weeks.

I had become a broken, empty shell.

I was unable to walk and had a portable potty like the ones used in nursing homes right next to my bed, and I felt hopeless, anxious, depressed, and angry to a degree no one understood.

That was February—five weeks into my slow climb back up the ladder. I had hit the bottom rung during Kennedy's first Christmas (see "An Invitation to Be Famous at Home"). We were standing in my parents' guest room when Josh put his hands on my shoulders, looked me square in the eyes, and said, "I just want my wife back."[1]

I sobbed. I wanted to come back. When I lost myself during those early years of motherhood, my children—and my husband—saw the worst version of me in the history of Christi.

So much for being famous.

The question I had to ask myself on the bottom rung of life was, what kind of mark will I leave on those I love?

Could my kids trust me to show up? Could I trust *myself* to show up?

Those questions woke me up.

My husband got an irritable and distant wife, and my kids knew that Mommy was edgy and angry. I was resentful toward God for how difficult my life had become and consumed with chasing respite in anything that promised to numb the pain and quiet the noise.

Why is it that we often ignore or dismiss what we have but chase the things we don't have? That's true not only with our possessions, but also with our loved ones, our talents, and our deepest desires. I was living my dream of having a family but still found myself on the bottom rung of life, wishing I had it all together.

One of the myths of fame is that it's equivalent to having it all together. But the pressure can be unrelenting. Ask anyone who's famous and they'll tell you that being famous doesn't always feel good. It just means you always have eyes on you.

Read that last sentence again.

Fame means you always have eyes on you. That includes being famous at home. Your biggest fans follow your every move, including how you handle yourself when you don't feel good. And as pain, feelings of inadequacy, and difficult life circumstances pile up, so do the feelings of responsibility to do something about it. But too often, we go down the "do something about it" path alone. We chase. And as that chase begins, our mental and emotional energy shifts our attention away from our biggest fans.

Learning to Accept That Your Parents Are Human

JOSH

Most parents begin with sincere intentions. They want to be the best parents in the world to their kids. But somewhere along the way something in their own story keeps them chasing. One of the most challenging journeys of the human experience is the deep psychological and spiritual conflict of honoring our parents' sincere intentions of raising us well, while also recognizing how their chase of something else (money, a promotion, social status) or someone else (clients, fans, congregants, authority figures) wounded us.

This is a tension I'm learning to hold.

Because my dad was always in the stands at my wrestling

matches and baseball games and showed up outside to play with me in the pool, shoot hoops, and teach me to ride a motorbike, I didn't recognize how his chase influenced not only my childhood but also my life today. Not until I sat in that group therapy circle replaying the driveway scene did I realize how his inability to show up for me emotionally at important moments in my life influenced what I chase today.

Please don't misunderstand. At times, all of us will prioritize or chase something other than our family. The Bible assures us, "For everything there is a season" (Ecclesiastes 3:1). But I'm not talking about the one-off seasons when we need to start a business, launch a project, or go on a deployment. I'm talking about when chasing something or someone other than family becomes a lifestyle—the rule, not the exception.

When I speak of my dad's inability to show up for me, I don't mean that my dad was never emotionally present. I mean that in key moments of my life when I needed emotional safety, he, too, was searching for it, rendering him unable to give it. At ten years old, my own emotional safety wasn't a burden I was ready or equipped to carry.

I didn't begin to recognize what had happened until a few decades later when I first felt the effects of my own chasing, a pursuit that ultimately left me paralyzed by fear. In all transparency, it took me a while to admit that my dad was human, that he had faults. But it was in seeing his humanity that I could both honor him and acknowledge his shortcomings.

When I later looked at the generational patterns of the men who'd gone before my dad, I gained a new perspective, one that enabled me to honor my dad's resilience in showing up for me the way he did while also recognizing the generational patterns that influenced what he once chased.

It was only in acknowledging those patterns that I could choose to break them. Had I refused to see them, I might have had all the sincere intentions in the world to show up and be famous for my kids, but somewhere along the way, my own chasing would have caught up with me. I would have broken the trust my kids have that I'll show up in the critical moments when they need me most.

Honoring our parents is a biblical command. But true honor doesn't exist in denial. To honor well is to acknowledge the brokenness in our parents' journeys, to forgive them, and to reconcile where possible. If we deny or excuse the pain, we run the risk of carrying into our own family story the same generational patterns and hurt that kept them chasing.

There's no honor in that. Not for my parents or my grandparents.

To truly honor my dad as his biggest fan is not to deny the times he failed me but to heal and learn from those moments, to focus on what a resilient man he was in all the ways he did show up for me, and then to carry that forward in an even healthier way.

Raising the Floor for Your Biggest Fans

Though it may not always feel like it, your biggest fans live under your roof. And you have more influence on those little fans than on any other "followers" you'll ever gain. Many studies suggest that our children's emotional maturity and adult life satisfaction are connected to our emotional presence and how well we showed up as parents.[2] In other words, for our children to enter the world with emotional resilience, we first need to raise the ceiling of our own emotional maturity. Our emotional ceiling will be our children's emotional floor.

Don't let that scare you. Even if you find yourself on the bottom rung of life, the next rung is all you need to focus on. The trouble is that we often shift our focus away from the next rung and onto the ceiling. In other words, instead of setting one small goal, we get overwhelmed by everything we think we need to fix right now, believing the lie that we must have it all together. But when you stare at the ceiling from the floor, it looks farther away than it really is. And that distance can leave you feeling hopeless, ashamed, and looking for affirmation in other places.

As parents, we all want our children to follow us. To become like us. To share our values and love what we love. But somewhere along the way, often without realizing it, we start investing our time, money, and mental energy in getting *others* to "follow" or "like" us. We spend our limited resources on other fans because, if we're honest, they give us a more immediate return on our investment. They affirm the parts of us that are insecure. Love the parts of us that feel unlovable. Believe in us when we don't believe in ourselves.

Short-term dopamine bumps from fans outside the home can cause us to subtly turn our attention away from our fans within the home because our spouse and kids don't always make us *feel* famous. Our kids don't like doing what we grew up loving. Our spouse feels more like a roommate than a lover. Affections begin to shift.

Christi chased the false affirmation of social media.

I chased the affirmation of people who saw me as a "go-getter" and "the guy who gets things done."

Christi's chase led her to her iPhone.

My chase led me to work.

In both cases, our biggest fans, those vulnerable eyes under our roof, watched and felt our unhealthy ways of dealing with pain. That's because they got their heroes' leftovers.

To get to the next rung, Christi and I made an important

decision to increase our intentionality with our biggest fans—we surrounded ourselves with godly mentors, a therapist, and spiritually mature friends—investing time and money into our own lives to help us show up well for our biggest fans.

Raising your emotional ceiling isn't as daunting as it might seem. Climbing the ladder of emotional maturity happens one rung at a time as you shift your focus away from the ceiling and onto the next rung. What rung are you on right now? Where do you feel unseen? In what ways are you trying to get others to follow you, to like you, to see you, to fill that void? What's keeping you stuck on that rung?

Every decision you make to keep climbing the ladder is a move toward being famous at home. The Bible says, "Parents are the pride of their children" (Proverbs 17:6). It's a promise that can be true for you, even if things at home aren't what you want them to be right now. Your kids are watching, and they're cheering you on.

4

YOUR BIGGEST ADVERSARY

What Shadows Keep You from Showing Up?

CHRISTI

The walls of my childhood bedroom in our one-level ranch-style home on Green Lane were covered in pink-and-white wide-striped wallpaper. Green Lane was appropriately named because our home in London, Ontario, sat under a canopy of giant pine and spruce trees so tall you couldn't see the tops of them. One of my biggest fears as a child came from the grand pine tree just outside my front bedroom windows. Its massive branches swayed in the wind, casting creepy dark shadows that danced across those delicate pink-and-white-striped walls. At night, those scary shadows became strangers coming to kidnap me through the window, or so a little girl's fear tells the story.

I learned to trust God in that little bedroom. He sat with me in the dark when the shadow strangers had me too scared to move a muscle. I whispered to him with my eyes squeezed shut, hiding under my cozy covers, the only protection between me and my ultimate safe haven, my parents' bedroom right across the hall. I am grateful to have learned to trust God at such a young age, amid dancing shadows on my bedroom walls.

As I grew up, my bedroom didn't change much. Never a fangirl type, I didn't decorate the walls with movie posters or other typical teen-girl obsessions. The only poster I ever put up was a long banner of three verses from Habakkuk. Strange for a teen girl, I'm sure, but something in the verses spoke to me:

> I will take my stand at my watchpost
>   and station myself on the tower,
> and look out to see what he will say to me,
>   and what I will answer concerning my complaint.
>
> HABAKKUK 2:1, ESV

The image of standing at my watchpost felt attractive, more empowering than waiting for the impending doom of the dancing dark shadows. I felt purpose and assurance in taking a stance of watching—waiting and alert rather than lying down and asleep. I read and reread those verses thousands of times within the pink-and-white-striped walls in the house on Green Lane. Apart from those shadows, I hadn't fought many battles in my life up to that point. Still, the room felt like God's training ground for battles yet to come.

I Have Enemies?

Battle isn't a concept I'm drawn to. Though I loved sports growing up and played college volleyball, I was never the competitive type. The team and sport itself attracted me far more than the glories of winning. I'd rather hand out trophies like candy and avoid conflict. But life doesn't work like that. We have enemies. And if we have enemies, we will have battles.

The Bible tells us to expect battle, to train for it, and to be ready for it in and out of season. That's where the image of being a watchman comes into play. In biblical times, watchmen were guards stationed on the high walls or watchtowers of a town or military fortress. From their elevated position, these sentries could see far into the distance and keep watch for any sign of approaching threats. While the Bible contains many references to actual watchmen who looked for physical threats, watchmen are also referred to in a spiritual sense.[1]

Old Testament writers described how God appointed prophets to oversee the souls of his people. Being a spiritual watchman was a heavy responsibility, requiring vigilance and obedience to the call. New Testament writers referred to church leaders as overseers, accountable to God to watch over the souls of those they shepherded. We might call them spiritual watchmen. But the role of a watchman isn't limited to prophets and church leaders.[2] As spouses and parents, we have the responsibility and high calling of being watchmen and watchwomen over our families, positioned in high places of prayer where *our eyes* are vigilantly trained on the horizon, *our ears* are listening for the voice of God concerning our loved ones, and *our attention* is on alert for any sign of approaching threat.

Our primary enemy, whom Jesus referred to as a thief and a wolf, prowls the earth with only one goal, "to steal and kill and destroy" (John 10:10). I'm not being dramatic; those are Jesus' actual words: *steal, kill, destroy*. The challenge is that this enemy is invisible. And yet, what happens in the unseen realm is more real than the book you hold in your hands. If we could see that war raging and witness in real time the battles fought over you and me, our kids, our marriages, and the decisions we make, it would no doubt change how we pray. Knowing this, the enemy endeavors to keep us distracted, busy, fearful, or comfortable so we dismiss or turn a blind eye to what he's really doing—keeping us from living in abundance.

I grew up with a mum who was wise to such enemy tactics.

When I was a little girl, every Sunday we loaded the family into our gray minivan to make the twenty-minute drive across town to Wortley Baptist Church. Most Sundays, Dad, Mum, my sister, brother, and I exited the minivan with fake smiles plastered on our faces after surviving a drama-filled morning to get there. As siblings, we routinely fought during the week, but Sunday mornings were always the main event. I can't remember a Sunday I didn't lose my temper over an outfit Mum wanted me to wear but didn't fit right.

I asked my mum one terrible Sunday morning why it was always like this.

Calm and collected, she said, "Because the enemy doesn't want us to go to church. But we won't let him win."

I didn't know he cared that much about one little family attending church.

But he did. And he still does.

The enemy doesn't care much about the intimacy of your marriage being a five or lower on a scale of one to ten. He leaves well enough alone when we aren't a threat to him. But start living at a new level of faith and intimacy with God and each other and you'll likely begin seeing new dancing dark shadows as the enemy tries to keep you hiding under the covers. Thriving marriages threaten him. Being famous at home to your kids provokes him.

Why?

Because your thriving family is a weapon in heaven's army. As your children learn the Word of God and grow to trust the heart of the Father with their lives, they carry the sword of the Spirit and the shield of faith (Ephesians 6:16-17)—which is why the Bible tells us we're blessed when we fill our quivers (Psalm 127:5).

But somewhere along the way, when the dark shadows—busyness, financial difficulties, physical pain, relational brokenness, postpartum depression, colicky babies, unruly kids—appear too big to overcome, we find ways to hide under the covers rather than engage the battle. While there are seasons in life when retreat and survival must be the goal, there are dangers to remaining stuck in survival mode long after it's necessary.

Living too long in survival mode will eventually wear on your soul. With your eyes fixed on the shadows, you'll crawl deeper under your covers—social status, work, social media, food, money, or whatever your security blanket is. Coming out from under them feels too risky. So, you settle for what feels comfortable. You convince yourself that living at a five out of ten in your marriage is "fine" and "as good as it will get." You settle for a job in which you find little fulfillment because it's "worth it financially," even when it pulls you away from spending time with your kids. Or maybe you say yes to everyone around you under the cover of "serving others" or "being a blessing," while leaving your loved ones with your leftovers.

Friend, the enemy would love nothing more than to keep you believing your identity is found in anything else but God. The more he can keep you chasing, the more he can keep you from engaging. And less engagement at home, over time, will slowly and subtly create a growing relational divide between you and your biggest fans.

As a wife and momma who today stands on her watchpost for

her husband and kids, I look back with fondness on the days when I positioned myself as a "watchgirl" in prayer. I learned to silence the voice of the enemy when I stopped focusing on what the dark shadows could do *to* me and learned to pay attention instead to what the Light behind the shadows could do *for* me. Today, when I begin to feel emotionally distant from Josh, or I sense a disconnect with my kids, instead of going under my covers to feel safe and comfortable, I identify the shadows stalking our family and expose them to the Light.

Fear: The Antithesis of Feeling Loved

JOSH

On a warm spring day a few years ago, I connected with Matt, a guy whose wife had reached out to us for coaching the day before. Vanessa was desperate. But we only do marriage coaching if both spouses buy in. We can't coach someone who doesn't want to be coached.

I took Matt's call and walked outside. I like to pace around the front lawn on coaching calls. There's something about walking while talking that keeps me engaged. I also tend to remember more details of my conversations this way.

So I paced, listening to Matt's side of the story and looking for any semblance of willingness in his voice. I could tell in the first few minutes Matt was a coach's dream player. He was hungry. And like his wife, desperate.

One of the first questions we ask each spouse is where they see themselves in the marriage on a scale of one to ten. A ten says, "Our relationship couldn't be better." A one says, "We're on the verge of divorce." Vanessa was a two. Matt was a four.

As I continued to pace the front lawn, Matt told me his story. "Josh, I called because a coworker told me about your podcast. He said I should reach out. When I heard Vanessa had already talked to you, I knew God was trying to tell me something."

"Where do you feel most stuck?" I asked.

"In my marriage. And it's been like this for years," he said. "I feel like she resents me, and I have no idea how to change that. I want to, but all of my attempts fail. Nothing I do pleases her."

To get a better understanding of his story, I then asked for examples of how he serves her and how she dismisses him. But somewhere in his explanation, Matt's tone of voice shifted from blame toward Vanessa to shame toward himself. "I travel a lot for work. I'm gone a few days most weeks, and honestly, because it's been so difficult to connect with her, I struggle with pornography on the road. I know I don't come home in the same excited state of mind to see her when I give in to the temptation, so I know I could be doing better. I just can't seem to stop the cycle."

The journey of chasing fame—or feelings of significance—in the wrong places is as complex and as unique to each individual as their fingerprints. But for the sake of demonstrating what's at play here, I'm going to risk oversimplifying things.

We chase when we don't feel loved. Because when we don't feel loved or supported, fear starts following us. And fear is what keeps us chasing. Remember what the apostle John wrote about love and fear?

"Such love has no fear, because perfect love expels all fear. *If we are afraid, it is for fear of punishment*, and this shows that we have not fully experienced his perfect love" (1 John 4:18, emphasis added).

When we focus more on what the scary shadows could do *to* us than what the Light behind the shadows can do *for* us, we hide under our covers.

Christi felt alone in her postpartum depression. Her fear of being a terrible mother and wife left her feeling unlovable. So, she chased.

My fear of letting others down and therefore being without money to support our family had me saying yes to every opportunity that came my way. I had a career-defining moment when my friend John Townsend said to me, "Josh, I've known you for over ten years, and your biggest weakness is saying yes to every good opportunity. You leave yourself no room to discover the great." The fear of letting others down and being without money kept me chasing.

Matt didn't feel loved at home, so he chased work and pornography. He carried two competing fears that left him walking a tightrope of blame and shame.[3] The fear of being seen as inadequate or weak left him blaming his wife. The fear that people might leave him if they knew the real Matt, how he struggled with pornography, kept him in shame—alone and beating himself up.

Vanessa didn't feel loved and feared Matt's constant rejection. Her chase for significance and security took the form of hard work and caring for their kids. Together, she and Matt ran multiple businesses. Although they had become great work partners, they had also become horrible lovers.

When you don't feel supported, your fears of being abandoned, unloved, or insignificant keep you chasing after other sources of significance or stability. As the antithesis of love, it's fear that follows you. If there is one thing the enemy wants to do, it's getting you to believe that God isn't for you. That he doesn't love you. That your spouse resents you. And that you have to go through life alone.

The enemy will lie to you. He will accuse and shame you. Make you think that you're nothing but a terrible mom. A deadbeat or workaholic dad. Or, fill in the blank. You know exactly what he accuses you of. And when you come into agreement with that accusation, fear drives your insecurity and keeps you chasing, searching for a renewed identity.

But identity is never found outside of community. And though I'll share more about Matt and Vanessa's story later, Matt's courage in making that first phone call was a game changer for him. Pacing across the front lawn, I was all in for Matt. I saw in him what he didn't see in himself. He needed a source of love and support to help him begin chasing his wife in a new way—not from fear, but from love.

As you consider your own life and the shadows you face, where do you see yourself? What shadow keeps you from showing up? Is it busyness, fear, self-doubt, financial difficulties, physical pain, relational brokenness, postpartum depression, a colicky baby, unruly kids? What cover do you use to keep you safe from the shadows? Is it social status, work, social media, food, money, pornography, notoriety? Do you spend more time hiding under the covers or standing on your watchpost? Is praying for your family as much a priority as scrolling through social media?

I ask these questions not to make you feel guilty or ashamed but to wake you up to the reality of what's going on around and within the hearts of your biggest fans. When you're fully awake and alert on your watchpost, you'll be better equipped to answer questions like these:

- What threats have I recognized coming into our kids' lives?
- What dangers are on the horizon for our marital intimacy?
- What shadows have we allowed to stick around, keeping our family from living on purpose?
- What is God saying to us about the direction of our family?

When you don't feel loved, fear will keep you chasing and pull you away from your watchpost—leaving your family without the care and protection that only you can provide. The focus you put on your own chase makes it much more difficult to recognize how the enemy is subtly attempting to steal, kill, and destroy your family. You might miss the sadness in your child's heart from being rejected by friends, the ongoing loneliness your spouse feels at home or at work, or the impact of the ever-increasing activities that have everyone going their separate ways but never together.

Getting back on your watchpost and exposing your shadows to the Light is a process, and it doesn't happen overnight. It's an ongoing journey of learning to trust again, being vulnerable with one another, and learning how to fight on behalf of the hearts of your biggest fans. But when you do, the love you give and the love you feel changes everything.

5

YOUR SIGNIFICANCE

How Is Your Identity Guiding Your Family?

JOSH

As a public speaker, I live in the conference scene. When I attend conferences, I enjoy meeting new people and having dinner with old friends. Years ago, if I wasn't actively attending or being invited to speak at a conference, my ego would take a hit. Especially if I saw other friends speaking at those events. It was my version of FOMO (fear of missing out). Instead of being excited about the event and my friends' opportunities, I often felt sorry for myself, sad I wasn't invited or able to attend.

But then I had children—a little boy and girl who longed for my attention. And a wife who wanted—okay, needed—me at home. If I wanted to live the very messages I spoke about onstage, I had to spend more time at home.

It's not that I didn't want to be home. I love playing with my kids. And I really do enjoy being with my wife. But for the decade that preceded having a family, my primary source of affirmation came from what I did, how I helped others, and the connections I enjoyed making.

I'll never forget the day that dynamic began to shift for me.

I had decided to work a few hours one Friday morning and then take the rest of the day to be with the family. Our kids' love for Thomas the Tank Engine meant I'd be building a track and visiting the Island of Sodor that afternoon. Sitting on the play-room floor, I briefly scrolled through Instagram and saw friends at various events across the country. It was conference season. People were on the go. And I was sitting on our playroom floor hauling around small plastic trees and other decorations so my kids could throw a birthday party for Percy, one of the youngest tank engines on Sodor. I can't remember if one of the kids asked me to do something or if I just "woke up," but I got up, took my phone into the other room, turned it off, and left it there.

It was time to stop chasing.

Every night as I tuck our kids into bed, I ask them to tell me about their favorite part of the day. On this night, though, before I could even ask, my four-year-old boy beat me to it.

"Daddy, what was your favorite part of today?"

As I took a few seconds to think, my eyes began to fill with tears.

"Buddy," I answered, "it was playing Thomas the Tank Engine with you and having a birthday party for Percy."

I meant it, too. That answer wasn't just lip service. I walked out of his bedroom knowing I'd had more fun playing with my kids that day than if I'd been at any of the conferences I'd seen on Instagram.

For a decade prior to getting married, I had attached my identity and significance to what I did and to what others thought of my hard work. But as I sat on my boy's bed, my identity began to shift. Though I would have agreed intellectually with the statement, "My biggest fans live under my roof," it wasn't until I spent time with my kids on the Island of Sodor that I began to feel alignment between my soul and my mind.

We don't show up well at home . . .

when we confuse who we are with what we do.

when we confuse who we are with what we haven't yet accomplished.

when we confuse who we are with what others have said about us.

when we confuse who we are with who we hang out with.

when we confuse who we are with the invitations we do or do not receive.

when we confuse who we are with how much money we make.

My journey to becoming famous at home started with reprioritizing my roles. I couldn't just give lip service to things like, "I love God, my spouse, my kids, and my work—in that order." Did I really? By reading comments and DMs while playing with my kids? By incessantly checking emails? By justifying reasons I couldn't have a date night with my spouse?

In recognizing what keeps you from being truly present with your loved ones, you'll likely discover the things to which you attach your significance. That's why the foundation for becoming famous at home is a matter of identity—knowing who you are and knowing who your family is.

Knowing Who You Are

Following the beautiful afternoon of Percy's birthday party, I spent the next few years exploring who I was without reference to my work. I wanted to rediscover the fun-loving ten-year-old Josh who would have enjoyed going to the creek that hot July day instead of taking on the responsibility of his parents' divorce. And I wanted to learn how to allow myself to be loved again by my heavenly Father, not because of what I could do for him but simply because he loves me for who I am—his child.

Even though I had followed Jesus most of my life and knew much of this in my head, it wasn't until I began to untether myself from the world's definition of significance that God's love began to settle into my heart. It's a journey I'm still walking out one day at a time.

One of the biggest struggles I have in a fast-paced, entitled, "fix my problem now" Western world is the temptation to ask God for what I think I need for my *doing* rather than what I really need for my *being*. And when I do that, I act like a teenager who runs home for a quick bite to eat, yells a courtesy, "I love you," to my parents from the kitchen, and runs back out the door to find my identity in the world. All the while, Mom and Dad sit in the living room just waiting to spend time with me.

To attach my identity to my *being*—to who I am in God—I had to pursue my relationship with God more than I pursued invitations to events. I had to spend time with him before I did anything else in my day. In my experience, showing up for my biggest fans happens in its purest form when I feel loved by God. I think it's why the apostle John wrote, "We love each other because he loved us first" (1 John 4:19). Anytime I look for love elsewhere, I'm let down. It's also when I chase fame or significance in the wrong places.

My identity as a child of God changes how I show up in my roles on earth. All the other sources to which I try to attach my identity ultimately become burdens that keep me enslaved to the chase. But being a son of God makes me an heir (Galatians 4:7), and then my obedience flows out of the love he gives to me. Job titles no longer matter to me. Speaking engagements, conferences, or times away for work are now filtered through the lens of how my travel impacts every member of our family. The measure of my success and significance is no longer about winning approval but whether I'm making an impact for eternity (Galatians 1:10).

As someone who had become immersed in a world enamored with position, social status, and advancement, these were monumental shifts for me. And one of the most significant parts of my journey was stepping into my own story, saying goodbye to identities that no longer served me well, and grieving what I was giving up. Because what's birthed from a recognition of what we lose is gratitude for what we gain. I might have lost what seemed like good opportunities to the world, but what I gained was a deeper connection with my kids on the Island of Sodor. And in an upside-down way, the joy I experienced in the smaller moments with my kids actually allowed me to show up with more joy and confidence in the seemingly grander moments on stage. Being famous at home helped me to show up as a truer version of myself in all I'm called to do.

Our presence in the moment is one of the greatest gifts we can give to one another—and to ourselves. But we first must learn to say no to the identities that rob us of our ability to be present in the moment. You know what's driving you. Stealing your time. Distracting your attention. Whenever you say yes to one thing, you say no to something else. And when your family gets the brunt of the no, there's likely something out of place.

When we named our organization Famous at Home, we did so knowing it had a dual meaning—that we wanted to be famous not only in our earthly home but also in our heavenly home. At the end of our lives, we want nothing more than to know we have lived a life worthy of trust—that God trusted us to show up for him, and our family trusted us to show up for them. Everything else is just icing on the cake.

That's because the fame we chase here is perilous. In fact, a friend of ours, a husband and dad who is well known in his field, told us one of his biggest prayers for his kids is that they never experience fame. You don't have to look far to see how fame's unrelenting pressures and idols can destroy a marriage, a family, a congregation, or a business. But that's the selfish, earthly version of fame. There is also a selfless version of fame—one the Bible includes with its own list of people who lived out this kind of fame.

The writer of the book of Hebrews introduces us to these people, made famous by their faith, saying, "Through their faith, the people in days of old earned a good reputation" (Hebrews 11:2). These were everyday people who struggled with sin just as you and I struggle. But one trait set them apart from their contemporaries—their faith in God. In other words, they knew who they were and to whom they belonged.

> They agreed that they were foreigners and nomads here on earth. . . . But they were looking for a better place, a heavenly homeland. That is why God is not ashamed to be called their God, for he has prepared a city for them.
>
> HEBREWS 11:13, 16

These everyday people became heroes of the faith because they were determined to live not for fame on earth but for fame in their heavenly homeland. The promise of Hebrews 11 is that this kind of fame is more than attainable for all of us because God "rewards those who sincerely seek him" (Hebrews 11:6).

Being famous in our earthly home comes from having faith that we already are significant in our heavenly home. That kind of faith not only helps us to know who we are as individuals but also helps us to know who we are as a family.

Knowing Who Your Family Is

CHRISTI

Those who live their earthly lives to be famous in heaven look different from those who live to be famous on earth. I've met a few such people, and their very presence is disarming. These are people who live *from* God's love, not *for* his love, and who find their identity as a family because of that love.

Two of these humans are my great-uncle Keith and great-aunt Myrtle—an uncelebrated, ordinary couple known for their faithfulness. Today, they live in a residential facility for retired missionaries. Nothing fancy, but they don't mind.

In the early years of their marriage, they committed their lives to doing hard and unseen acts of faith, moving their family to live deep in the Amazon jungle of Brazil with a people group who had no written language and who had never seen a white person, let alone trusted one. Uncle Keith and Aunt Myrtle raised their children in that jungle, without access to modern medicine or conveniences, with the express purpose of loving people long enough to earn their trust and tell them about the God who loved them so much that he sent an average Canadian family to tell them so.

They lived a lifetime of hidden, unseen, uncelebrated faith. After decades in the jungle, they were so trusted by the Yanomami people that when the local men went to war against neighboring tribes, they left their possessions with Keith and Myrtle rather than with their family or friends.

After they retired and returned to Canada, the pastor of a small church once invited Uncle Keith to share about his years of ministry. As he finished telling stories about their time with the Yanomami people, the pastor, as if asking for a baseball score, asked how many converts he had. Uncle Keith looked down at the pulpit and quietly said, "None."

"Then it seems your ministry was a failure," the pastor curtly replied.

Uncle Keith never forgot those words. I've heard him say, "In the church's eyes, our ministry wasn't successful. But I know we did it because the Lord asked us to. I have to remember that."

I hope I never have to meet that spiteful pastor. I'd kick him in the shins.

In one sentence, with his misguided understanding of fame and earthly chasing, he tried to steal the joy of a lifetime of humble love. But isn't that just what the enemy does—he flips the truth upside down and spews out spiteful lies about the insignificance of our lives and our callings. He makes us question our God-given purposes—as individuals and as a family. And he uses other human beings to do it, including modern-day Pharisees such as that pastor.

Fortunately, that's not the end of the story. Building on the foundation of trust established by his parents, Keith and Myrtle's son decided to remain in the jungle. And what neither that pastor nor Uncle Keith knew at the time was how their son would see many Yanomami come to faith. The seeds you sow as a parent may not bear fruit in your season, but that doesn't mean you haven't left a legacy. A true legacy is when you know who your family is and you choose to remain faithful, regardless of the outcome.

When you know your identity as a son or daughter of God, your worth as a person no longer rises and falls on being a stay-at-home parent, mompreneur, CEO, musician, service member, speaker, laborer, podcaster, or whatever roles you might hold. Instead, you live *from* love, not *for* love. You can show up *for* your family, not just *with* your family. Living from love as a child of God makes knowing who your family is, and what God calls you to as a family, much easier. Because you no longer have anything to prove.

Our job on earth is to bring God glory in how we lead our family, love others, and make choices—both big and small, seen and unseen. And when we do that, we, too, can leave legacy upon legacy to our children and our children's children. Not because of anything flashy we do but because our kids learn that God is a living, breathing heavenly Father whose love for us changes how we show up for others.

God is looking for humble hearts who will lay down their lives to realize his Kingdom on earth a little more each day, regardless of the cost or how hidden our contribution might be. That's what it means to know who your family is—to identify the ways in which you can partner with God to advance the Kingdom. For Keith and Myrtle, that meant serving as missionaries in a remote Brazilian village. For Josh and me, that means bringing a renewed sense of connection, adventure, and purpose to families. For you, that means discovering the heartbeat and identity of your family and then living it out. And we'll walk you through a process to do just that with the Seven Decisions in part 3.

As you discover more about who you are and who your family is, it might require making some changes in your lifestyle, job, schooling for your kids, or even where you live. But don't be afraid of reprioritizing your roles or even what God might call you to do as a family. Though change can feel scary in the moment, imagine what God can do through your family on the other side of your faith. As Dale Mast writes, "Faith believes what God can do. Identity believes what God can do through you."[1] Let your faith guide you. Let your identity guide your family.

A Supernatural Perspective

JOSH

Because I didn't grow up in a charismatic church, I was skeptical when I encountered other Christians who spoke prophetic words over my life. Over the years, I learned to take a wait-and-see approach. When someone offered a prophetic word about my life, I wrote it down and put it on a shelf. If their word came to pass, then I knew that person was a voice I could trust.

However, there was no wait-and-see required the day Pastor Aaron Smallwood spoke words of prophecy over me for the first time. Christi and I had just showed up to our first house church meeting hosted by some new friends. Already hesitant, we showed up late, which was awkward. To add awkward to awkward, we walked in just as a pastor was prophesying over people.

Standing among a circle of white couples was a regal black man dressed in a priestly robe. Christi and I joined the circle, and it wasn't long before Pastor Smallwood approached me, asking and getting my permission to prophesy.

"Did you have a mentor?" he asked.

My mind went back through the years. The examples that came to mind were the not-so-good ones.

"Good or bad?" I asked.

"I get the sense this is someone who really influenced your life. He's also someone who isn't with us anymore."

My eyes instantly filled with tears. Christi grabbed my hand.

"Yes," I said, "my dad died seven months ago."

Before Pastor Smallwood continued, he paused and took a few steps back. Nothing could have prepared me for what he said next.

"I see an angel standing right next to you holding a sword," he said. "It is so bright and fierce looking I'm afraid to get too close."

Whoa! What did he just say?

Not sure what to do or say, I just smiled, tears still in my eyes.

"Josh," Pastor Smallwood continued, "I get the sense this angel was sent to protect you in ways your dad wanted to but couldn't while he was here on earth. This angel was assigned to you, and God wants you to know that."

I was now speechless in my tears. This moment opened my eyes to a whole new perspective on what might be going on in the unseen world around us. This man knew nothing about me or my story before we awkwardly entered the circle that day. As I mentioned before, my dad had always been in the stands when I was growing up. He loved me fiercely. But I always had a sense he wished he could have been emotionally stronger for me in my vulnerable moments. Now, this man I had never met was filling my life with a double dose of love from both my heavenly Father and my earthly dad.

Talk about finding significance. In that moment, I felt so loved. Fought for. Seen. I knew there was eternal significance to who God had called our family to be. And I feel like my dad is as much a part of that journey now as he was when he walked the earth.

I could fill a book with stories such as this one describing experiences Aaron and Christi and I have had and how God confirms over and over again how much he cares about the details of our lives.

As you reflect on your understanding of who you are and who your family is, ask yourself two questions:

- What roles might God be asking me to reprioritize so I can live more joyfully from who I am and be more fully present with others?
- What purpose might God have for our family that is bigger than us?

Then ask one more question, perhaps the most important question of all: "Do I believe God loves me enough to fight for me and guide my family, even in the tiniest of details?"

I believe God deeply loves you. He is fighting for you. He is guiding your family in ways both seen and unseen. You are that significant.

PART 2

AN OVERNIGHT SUCCESS A DECADE IN THE MAKING

JOSH

Though I am no Ron Burgundy, I do have a sign-off I use on every episode of our Famous at Home podcast: "Keep in mind, the greatest red carpet you'll ever walk is through your front door." That sign-off puts a bow on part 1, where we defined what it means to be famous at home and the journey each of us is on to find fame.

Though our life's path might not lead us to the Oscars or the Golden Globes, we all have red carpets—the places in life where we are seen and celebrated. We also have red carpets we chase, the ones on which we strive to be seen. But to be famous at home is to recognize that the greatest red carpet you'll ever walk is through your front door. Your kids sprinting to greet you as your biggest fans. Your spouse, the president of your fan club, beaming with pride not too far behind. And your grand entrance can happen every day when those you love jockey to be the first to greet you.

The image of walking a red carpet keeps me grounded and reminds me how I want to show up at home. Wearing my relational best. Grateful. Prepared. Arms wide open. Full of love. It is this posture of showing up with intentionality that leads us into the theme of part 2, "Becoming an Overnight Success a Decade in the Making."

Most successful people in business, entertainment, and sports will tell you that there is no such thing as an overnight success. Instead, what passes for "instant" fame is built on years of dedicated effort, practice, and tenacity. In part 2, that's our focus—the daily perseverance required for your next decade.

If that sounds overwhelming, keep in mind that positioning your family center stage means you're building relationships, not products. Nurturing souls, not programming robots. Playing with, not for, your biggest fans. It's a process that requires a long-term approach to showing up.

These next three chapters may very well be the most important chapters you read. The principles in part 2 help you build the foundation you'll need to implement the Seven Decisions over the next decade. They provide the "why" that enables you to sustain the "how" of the Seven Decisions. When you understand the why behind the Seven Decisions, you'll be equipped to keep showing up on the red carpet day after day, even when your kids throw a fit or both you and your spouse are at your wits' end. Like someone who is color-blind putting on corrective glasses and seeing color for the first time, you will see your marriage and your parenting through a new set of lenses.

6

ARE YOU WILLING?

Fame Chases Those Who Act

JOSH

John 5 tells the story of Jesus healing a paralyzed man who was lying beside the Pool of Bethesda, which was known for its miraculous healing powers. It's a fascinating story, particularly because of a question Jesus poses.

> One of the men lying there had been sick for thirty-eight years. When Jesus saw him and knew he had been ill for a long time, he asked him, "Would you like to get well?"
>
> "I can't, sir," the sick man said, "for I have no one to put me into the pool when the water bubbles up. Someone else always gets there ahead of me."
>
> Jesus told him, "Stand up, pick up your mat, and walk!"
>
> JOHN 5:5–8

Can you imagine asking a man who's been paralyzed for thirty-eight years if he wants to get well? Wouldn't the answer to that question seem obvious? So why did Jesus ask the paralyzed man if he wanted to get well? Perhaps because the answer wasn't as obvious as it seemed, and Jesus knew that.

Like his body, the man's identity had also been paralyzed. Just imagine all the unknowns of being able to walk when you hadn't walked for thirty-eight years. Being healed might actually have been something the man feared as well as desired. Being stuck on the edge of the pool might have felt a whole lot safer than being healed.

A similar dynamic can happen when we get stuck in marriage; it's often easier to stay stuck than it is to risk doing something to get unstuck. The unknowns of what we must do to move from a five to an eight on the marriage intimacy continuum can feel either overwhelming or not worth the effort.

"At least I know what I'm going to get with my spouse," we reason. Or maybe things are going well enough to be comfortable and we like being comfortable. "Why rock the boat? What good will it do to bring up stuff that just doesn't need to be talked about?"

So we maintain the status quo, living in a paralyzed relationship, not really wanting to stand or pick up our mat, both of which are prerequisites to walking forward in our relationships.

Remember Matt and Vanessa? When Vanessa first called me to inquire about marriage coaching, she told me all about Matt. How she had such a difficult time connecting with him. How he hurt her. And why she resented him for it. I heard a lot about Matt.

That's the case with most of the calls I receive. No matter which spouse initiates the first call, the answer to nearly every question I ask is about the other spouse. That's because when we hurt, we blame. We put up walls around our heart. We vow to not get hurt like that again. But when we self-protect, we stay stuck.

That's why I had to ask Vanessa a question similar to the one Jesus asked that paralyzed man.

"Are you willing?"

At Famous at Home, we help spouses get unstuck by casting a vision for their future as a couple. That's part of what distinguishes marriage coaching from therapy. In therapy, if one spouse is unwilling to get well, the other spouse can do individual therapy to heal parts of his or her past. In fact, if your spouse is hostile or abusive, trying to implement the strategies we teach could leave you even more exposed to ridicule and putdowns. Nobody should be subjected to emotional abuse. If this is you, we strongly suggest seeking therapy for yourself first. Marriage coaching requires two individuals who want to get well and who are willing to look to the future and set goals together.

Here are some of the questions I ask about willingness during that first call:

- "If I were to ask your spouse where he/she would rate your marriage on a scale of one to ten, what do you think the number would be?"
- "Does your husband/wife know you set up this call today?" About 50 percent of the time the answer is no. I then ask, "Why not?"
- "On a scale of one to ten, how willing do you think your spouse is to take your marriage to the next level?"
- "Can you get your spouse to take the initiative to set up a call with me this week?"

By the end of these questions, I usually have a pretty solid read on whether the couple is a good fit for marriage coaching or whether I need to refer the spouse or the couple for therapy.

If the other spouse reaches out to set up a follow-up call, it's akin to the paralytic man standing up—an affirmation that he or she is willing to be well and is courageous enough to take action.

Fortunately, Matt took the initiative to set up a call. And I could tell by our first conversation that he was willing to get unstuck.

To be willing might sound easy. You made it this far into the book because you're willing to do what it takes to be famous at home. You want a better marriage, you don't want to settle, and you want to move up a few notches on the one-to-ten marriage intimacy scale. You want more joy. You want to feel safe with your spouse and be more sexually intimate with each other. You want to connect more deeply with your kids and champion their hearts.

And yet, being willing isn't easy at all. It's one thing to say we're willing to experience each of the aforementioned ideals and another thing entirely to act on that willingness. The couples and families we work with who stay stuck don't lack for knowing what to do; they lack a willingness to apply what we coach them to do. Fame doesn't chase those who stop at knowing what to do; fame chases those who do it. And what keeps us stuck is often an unwillingness to do one or more of these four things: to give up blame, to pay the price of intimacy, to change the only person we can (ourselves), or to pray.

As you read the rest of the chapter, ask yourself what might keep you from being willing to do these four things. Is it fear of losing your voice in the relationship? Fear of getting hurt all over again? Fear of having to give more of yourself when you feel like there's nothing else to give? Fear of making a change that isn't enough for your spouse? Fear of not knowing how or what to pray? Invite the Holy Spirit to speak to you and hold on to the promise that "perfect love expels all fear" (1 John 4:18).

Are You Willing to Give Up Blame?

Dr. David Burns is a pioneer in cognitive-behavioral therapy, a drug-free treatment for depression and anxiety that has become the most widely used and extensively researched form of psychotherapy in history. As part of his work, he set out to research the attitudes that lead to happy and unhappy marriages—and what he found was eye-opening.[1]

According to his research, the key to a healthy, growing marriage came down to one big factor: How you feel in your marriage "depends entirely" on your own attitude, not the attitude of your spouse.[2] I may need to give you a moment to let that sting.

I routinely witness the truth of Burns's finding in our work coaching couples. The person making the initial call often spends most of the conversation telling us what's wrong with his or her spouse. That's what Vanessa did when she called. Instead of focusing on her part in their troubled marriage, she focused on Matt. Was Matt at fault? Sure. But not for everything. Just as your spouse isn't at fault for everything in your marriage either.

Every marriage story has three sides. Your side. Your spouse's side. And the truth. The way to the truth, which you'll learn in the next two chapters, begins when both individuals are willing to stop the blame game and take responsibility for their role in the conflict.

Though blame might seem like a reasonable option, especially when you've been hurt, it may be the number one culprit keeping you stuck—not just in your marriage, but in other relationships as well. Here's what Burns found:

> People who blamed their partners (or people in general) for the problems in their relationships were angry, frustrated, unhappy, and intensely dissatisfied with

> their relationships. In addition, this mind-set accurately predicted what would happen in the future. Individuals who blamed their partners for the problems in their relationship were even more miserably unhappy three months later.[3]

In full transparency, this is where Christi and I get stuck in our own marriage. Not so much in blaming each other but in a more subtle form of blame—which is refusing to give up our right to be right when we feel like we've been wronged. Christi and I are both firstborn, type A personalities who love to be right. When we get stuck, surrendering our right to be right is a tough pill for both of us to swallow.

Perhaps you are beginning to see why marriage coaching and relationship skills don't matter much if a couple isn't willing to give up assigning blame. Coaching skills require empathy and a genuine interest in understanding the underlying motivation behind your spouse's actions and words. But if you have already assigned meaning to your spouse's motivation, you won't listen to or care about anything they have to say. Instead, you'll either go on the offensive to even the score or go on the defensive to avoid more pain.

Here's something that may surprise you. Giving up blame also includes giving up self-blame. Just because you no longer blame your spouse (or your kids, for that matter) doesn't mean you go to the other extreme of beating yourself up or being a martyr. Both others-blame and self-blame can keep you stuck in a victim mentality. Others-blame keeps your spouse on the defensive; self-blame keeps you paralyzed. In both cases, your spouse is unable to share his or her feelings with you as an adult. If that sounds complicated, here's a story that demonstrates what it looks like in everyday life.

When Micah, our youngest, was about three months old, he wasn't sleeping or nursing well. With all three of our kids, I took every opportunity to be up with them through the night. Christi was a rock star mom. With Micah, she did everything she could to breastfeed, pump, and get Micah to latch. It was a constant back-and-forth to lactation consultants, chiropractors, and tongue-tie specialists. Not to mention the fact that she was homeschooling the two older kids and recording podcast episodes for Famous at Home. Getting up at night with Micah was the least I could do.

One night was especially rough. I was frustrated at how much Micah was awake. Bringing him to my side of the bed to change his diaper at about 3:30 in the morning, I let out a massive sigh of frustration. As soon as I did, I could feel the tension coming from Christi as she sat pumping on the other side of the bed. If you've been married long enough, nothing needs to be said to feel the weight of tension in the room after one of those sighs. It was heavy. Here's a bonus tip if you have an infant—nothing good ever comes out of an argument in the middle of the night, so it's best to just finish what you're doing and go back to sleep (if you can).

The tension was still there the next morning as Christi came downstairs. Instead of ignoring the issue and hoping it would just go away, I asked how she was doing.

"Josh," she said with a defensive posture and tone, "I'm doing everything I can. I'm sorry last night was a rough night, but I was unable to help."

That was it. She thought I was blaming her for the rough night and not being able to get the baby to sleep because she was pumping. And you see what she did? She tried to take responsibility for my frustrated feelings with self-blame—acting as if, in addition to pumping, she should be the one trying to get him back to sleep.

I walked over and took her by the hand. "Christi," I said, looking into her eyes, "I'm not blaming you for not helping with Micah, nor should you take this on as something you need to do. You're crushing it as a mom. That was my responsibility last night anyway, not yours. Can we do something from now on? Can we start treating each other like adults instead of trying to take responsibility for the other's emotions? Can you allow me to be frustrated at a bad night without trying to do anything about it or take responsibility for it?"

It was an eye-opening moment for two recovering co-dependents.

When we self-blame, we don't allow the other person to have feelings. It's too uncomfortable. So, in our own emotional discomfort, we try to sabotage the other person from feeling because we can't stand bearing the weight of it.

This is what happens with virtually every form of blame—you can't stand bearing the weight of the pain, so you off-load it with blame. If you blame your spouse, it takes the spotlight off you. If you blame yourself, it's akin to throwing a pity party, asking your spouse to ignore his or her painful feelings to ease the burden of the situation for you. Giving up blame is difficult because when you take responsibility, it requires getting out of your comfort zone and taking action to change things. And change rarely feels easy at the start.

Are You Willing to Pay the Price of Intimacy?

Moving up the scale of marital intimacy comes with a cost. We can't get well or move forward without being willing to do hard things. And paying the price of intimacy is one of those hard things. In his extensive research on overcoming barriers to intimacy, David Burns found that it is our willingness to endure the pain, or uncomfortable emotions, of getting close to the one we love that leads to intimacy.[4]

I had to be willing to pay the price of getting close to Christi's feelings and ask her how she was doing. For us to get unstuck, she had to be willing to endure my feelings of frustration without trying to fix them. None of us can grow in intimacy without inquiring about emotion. Many couples get stuck because one person feels overwhelmed by the other person's emotion. And when you don't know what to do with your spouse's emotion, the gut reaction is to defend yourself, shut down the other person, or go play video games. Or golf. Or go shopping. Or, well, you get picture. There are an endless number of ways to suppress emotion and walk away from intimacy.

Nobody likes conflict at the time. But when conflict is resolved in a healthy way, it leads to deeper intimacy. Consider your own willingness to endure the not-so-good feelings of getting close to your spouse. When are you most likely to get defensive? Is it around a particular topic? An accusation against you? When you feel insecure or exhausted? What topics do you steer clear of to avoid arousing negative emotions? In a conflict, is your initial reaction to blame and defend, or are you able to stop and consider your role in the conflict?

Perhaps you're beginning to see why it's necessary to address the issue of willingness before getting into the Seven Decisions. Recognizing what keeps you unwilling to pursue your spouse's heart with all your heart is where you will find fuel to make those decisions—to follow through when change is hard. Otherwise, you might know in your head what you need to do, but you won't be able to *will* yourself to do it. For now, just remember that the price you pay for intimacy in the moment will be pennies compared to the decades-long return on your relational investment.

Are You Willing to Change the Only Person You Can?

According to David Burns, we have three options in a difficult relationship:

> We can maintain the status quo and keep trying to change the other person.
>
> We can leave the relationship, because that's always an option.
>
> We can take responsibility to change the only person we can—ourselves.[5]

Just as Burns found others-blame to be the most crippling mindset in marriage, he found that taking personal responsibility to solve the problems in the relationship was the key to a happy, loving, and satisfying marriage. And the same principle extends to other relationships as well. Individuals who *assume responsibility for their role in the relationship and see it as their priority to make the other person happy* hold the two greatest keys to a rewarding, successful relationship over the long haul.[6] As Burns poignantly concludes, "Personal responsibility, without any blame at all, is the mind-set that leads to intimacy."[7]

Can you imagine how your marriage might be different if both you and your spouse took sole responsibility for how you act in conflict? Christi and I have struggled with this, especially when our kids were smaller. Like so many couples, we judged the actions of our spouse through our own lenses. You've already seen how I did that with thinking I was a bag of chips and then some by getting up through the night with the kids. What I missed was how depleted Christi was. Instead of stepping into her shoes and seeing our conflict through her struggles, I saw her attitude and accusations through my foggy glasses—one lens focused on how she didn't notice my efforts, and the other focused on how ungrateful she was for all I was doing.

Time to remove the log from your own eye there, Straub.

In Jesus' Sermon on the Mount, he said, "The standard you use in judging is the standard by which you will be judged. And why worry about a speck in your friend's eye when you have a log in your own?" (Matthew 7:2-3). Even though Christi is my best friend in the whole world, my instinctive reaction isn't to defend her when we argue. However, I'm learning that when I close my eyes for even a brief second to focus on that log, it reminds me of my responsibility to first change myself by owning my actions. Then I can step into Christi's world with more intentionality and concern.

Are You Willing to Pray?

"Are you willing to pray?" Depending on who I'm talking to and their own faith background, this is a question I ask from the very beginning. That's because every time we start coaching a couple, we see spiritual warfare increase. Something usually comes up that shifts the family's attention away from increasing the intimacy and quality of the marriage. Finances mysteriously take a hit. Someone gets sick. An unexpected work project requires one spouse to be away for a while.

Though we don't chalk up everything to spiritual warfare, the couples we see who make the most significant leaps in their intimacy together are willing to pray for and with their loved ones. They take seriously the enemy's desire to "steal and kill and destroy" (John 10:10). And yet, not everyone is willing to pray.

Some are afraid. They've never really prayed before and don't know what that looks like. Or they have prayed before, experienced increased spiritual warfare, and then retreated, resigning themselves to leave well enough alone. Others are ashamed. They've neglected prayer for so long they feel like failures in this department. I did.

But the enemy loves to use fear and shame to keep us stuck. Those willing to go to the next level of faith and spiritual growth for their family start by covering their family in prayer.

There's more happening around you than meets the eye.

A few years ago, Christi and I began turning to prayer whenever we felt exasperated with each other. You know those arguments so intense you both just resign in surrender? Instead of resigning and turning away from each other, we literally got on our knees in our home office and began praying. Sometimes I would lay hands on Christi. Other times she would lay hands on me. Instead of battling each other, we began to ask the question, "Lord, what else is at work here?"[8]

That question became a game changer for our marriage. The Holy Spirit revealed to us that our cycle of blame was often because we had allowed a spirit of fear into our relationship. Instead of calling it out, we fought each other. In most cases, whether those arguments were about the kids, finances, or the direction of our business, very little evidence existed to justify our issues with each other. It was just a spirit of fear leading to uncertainty, insecurity, and arguing.

Today, we refuse to allow conflict to paralyze us to the point of exasperation. Prayer is now our first line of defense. Similar to the paralytic man, we're not waiting on someone else to lift us into the pool of marital healing. We stand up, pick up our prayer mats, and walk toward healing together. We pray in the kitchen while we get coffee. We pray for each other with our kids wrapped around our legs in a family hug. We pray everywhere you could imagine. Why? Because when two people agree in prayer, they can be assured their Father in heaven is fighting for them (Matthew 18:19).

Remember, we have an enemy who loathes healthy, happy marriages that glorify God. If praying hasn't been your strong suit, that's okay. To help you get started with prayer, simply ask God to reveal to you how he sees your spouse. Write down what he shows you through his lens. As you make your list, ask him to help you start fighting for your spouse's heart the way he does. By being slow to get angry. Not dealing harshly or constantly accusing. Being filled with unfailing love (Psalm 103:8-10).

If you have trouble entering this posture toward your spouse, ask God to reveal what else might be at work. The shadows disappear when exposed to the Light. Some of the greatest breakthroughs in our marriage happened when I prayed despite what I was feeling toward Christi. You can lay your hands on and quietly bless your spouse or kids at any time. When your spouse is in need, ask how you can pray and do it right in the moment. It doesn't need to be anything fancy. You simply choose to act—because healing is on the other side of action.

I leave you with the same question Jesus asked the paralytic man: "Would you like to get well?" Are you willing to put your relationships at home center stage? If so, ask yourself, "Which mat do I need to pick up first? My blame mat—my willingness to stop blaming? My intimacy mat—my willingness to endure the uncomfortable emotions of getting closer to my spouse? My responsibility mat—my willingness to take responsibility for my actions? Or my prayer mat—my willingness to pray?"

Fame chases those who act and are willing to enter their loved ones' stories.

7

WHAT ARE YOU FIGHTING FOR?

Why Your Spouse Is Not Your Enemy

JOSH

Being a child of divorce, I wanted to choose well when it came to marriage. About four months into dating Christi, I took her as my plus-one to a buddy's wedding. What better way to figure out if she was the right one than to introduce her to some of my friends, right?

The wedding party spent the few days leading up to the ceremony getting to know one another and practicing a choreographed dance to the song "Jai Ho" from *Slumdog Millionaire*. It was epic.

Prior to our first dance practice, the groomsmen got together outside to play "500," a game in which a quarterback throws a football to a group of receivers at the other end of a field. The quarterback shouts a point value for each throw—50, 100, etc. Whoever catches the ball gets those points. The first receiver to reach 500 gets to be the quarterback.

When my reach for a ball fell short, it ended up bouncing off my pinky finger, and *yowzers*! Man, did it hurt. Thinking I had just jammed it, I stood there for a few seconds trying to pull it out. Besides, I was with the guys. No pain, no gain, right? My pride kept me in the game and I caught the next ball, which made me quarterback. But I was still fighting the pain and my first throw landed just a few feet in front of me. By now, the pain was excruciating.

I gave up on the game and walked into the house to get some ice. Christi was hanging with the bridal party and happened to be sitting right next to the refrigerator. Being Canadian, Christi grew up going to the skating rink to watch a fight, and every now and again a hockey game broke out. As I walked past her to get to the freezer, she asked, "Did you really hurt it, or are you just being a baby?"

I knew at that moment I was one step closer to my own wedding day.

She did too. Because when we arrived home a few days later, she found out she wasn't dating a baby. I had to see an orthopedic surgeon. I'd broken the pinky on the knuckle. Had I not had surgery—complete with pins sticking out of my pinky finger for the next few months—the bones would have fused together, and I would have been unable to bend my finger. For the rest of my life, I'd have been drinking tea with a straight pinky. Think Dr. Evil's-sinister-pinky-finger-to-his-mouth type of straight.

Fast forward to our wedding day. Christi's one request of me was, "Don't break anything." I promised I wouldn't.

The afternoon before our evening rehearsal, my soon-to-be father-in-law took the groomsmen to a place called Port Stanley, a beachfront along Lake Erie. While the groomsmen played volleyball and football on the beach, I sat on the sidelines talking through the ceremony with my best man and officiant, Shawn. At

4:20 p.m., Christi's dad walked over and said, "Guys, we have to leave in ten minutes to get ready for the rehearsal."

Thinking of Christi's request, I looked at Shawn and said, "What could happen in ten minutes?"

You might see where this is going.

Kicking off my shoes, I walked onto the beach. Shawn picked up a football and told my friend Brian—at whose wedding rehearsal I'd broken my pinky finger—to go out for a pass. My competitive nature had me defend Brian. The pass got broken up. This time, Christi's dad picked up the ball. "Last pass," he said, "then it's time to go."

Brian ran his route. I trailed behind, both of us barefoot. As his foot kicked back, my foot went forward, kicking him in the heel. I dropped like I'd been shot, my pinky toe on fire.

I told nobody. Jamming my foot into my shoe for the rehearsal and dinner that night, I battled for a normal gait. When I got back to the hotel and took off my shoe, the outside of my entire right foot was black. I'd broken my fifth metatarsal.

Were you nervous the night before your wedding? All I could think of was a pinky toe version of my pinky finger surgery, complete with pins sticking out, and the trip to Mexico we had planned for the day after our wedding.

After consulting with a few people who knew a bit about broken pinky toes, I was confident I didn't a need doctor for it to heal. I'd wear my dress shoe like a boot and try to pull off a "cool limp" every now and again. If ever there were a day to have a little swagger, this was it. I told everyone who knew to keep my broken toe a secret for our wedding day. Christi could not know! It was her one requested promise and I'd somehow managed to break it. Pun intended.

The morning after our wedding, I pulled Christi aside.

"Honey," I said, "I have a confession to make." Slipping off my shoe, I revealed the foot I'd been hiding from her. "I broke my pinky toe the day before our wedding."

She didn't miss a beat.

"Josh," she said, "you started our marriage on a foundation of lies."

And so began our journey to being famous at home.

Your Spouse Is Not Your Enemy

CHRISTI

Just as the serpent entered the Garden of Eden and deceived Adam and Eve with lies and seeds of doubt, the enemy is subtle and conniving in his efforts to undermine marriage. We both laughed on our honeymoon when I said Josh had started our marriage on a foundation of lies—and we've already agreed he has to wear a body cast the week leading up our kids' weddings. But in all seriousness, even if you don't carry lies into your marriage from the beginning, the enemy will do whatever he can to get you to believe lies about your spouse. And perhaps the sneakiest and most powerful lie of all is getting you to believe your spouse *is* the enemy.

Just as the serpent manipulated Adam and Eve into questioning God's character and motives, the enemy manipulates us into questioning the character and motives of our spouse. And just as Adam and Eve came into agreement with the serpent, we too, if we're not careful, can come into agreement with the enemy in believing lies about our spouse. When that happens, we're blinded to everything but our side of the story. The result is increased self-centeredness and emotional distance because we come to believe that it is our spouse, and not the enemy, who is out to get us.

The stories we tell ourselves about any given experience are colored by our history, our wounds, and our emotions. My therapist,

Mary, once said something to me I will never forget. "Christi, what's hysterical is often historical."[1] When our emotional reaction to a particular circumstance is disproportionate to that situation, it's likely a reaction to an unresolved hurt or fear from our past.

In marriage, when either the story I tell myself is different from the story Josh is telling himself, or I get so consumed by my own story that I'm unwilling to listen to his, I am one step away from assuming wrong motives on his part. Since my story makes logical sense to me, the only explanation in a disagreement must be that he is out to get me. If he's not fighting *for* me, he must be fighting *against* me. And since he's the enemy, I must protect my heart.

Over time, however, it's that very guarding of one's own heart from a spouse that creates a miserable marriage and sometimes leads to divorce. What do you think the greatest predictor of divorce might be? Lack of communication? Money problems? Reconnecting with a high school sweetheart on social media? Meddling in-laws? Difficult kids? Adultery?

In his extensive research on marriage and divorce, psychologist John Gottman found it to be none of these. It wasn't what the couple fought about that led to divorce. Instead, the greatest predictor of divorce was whether the couple remained emotionally connected despite their differences. When trouble came, the couples who turned their hearts away from each other divorced, but the couples who fought for each other's hearts stayed the course.[2]

One of the reasons we talk so much about emotions is because when there is conflict in marriage, the issue is almost never about the issue. The real issue is what's going on in your spouse's heart and whether you are willing to engage emotionally and seek understanding about the story your spouse is telling himself or herself. What's going on *within* your spouse's heart is more important than what's going on *between* the two of you.[3]

Solomon wrote, "Guard your heart above all else, for it determines the course of your life" (Proverbs 4:23). When we get married, we become one flesh with one marital heart to guard. And our willingness to endure the uncomfortable feelings of getting close to our spouse is what leads to greater connection, which is an essential component for a strong marriage.

So how do you begin fighting for your spouse's heart rather than fighting against each other? You name your opponent, call out the elephant in your marriage, and talk about your dance.

Name Your Opponent

Your spouse is not your enemy. Your spouse is your greatest ally and teammate when fighting the opponents to your marriage. Josh and I love sports and often use sports analogies in our own marriage. When trouble comes, we imagine ourselves in the same locker room putting together a game plan. If we get stuck or find ourselves fighting against each other, it's usually because we're in two different locker rooms, seeing the other as the opponent.

That's why one of your first assignments in moving up the marriage intimacy scale is to name your opponent. You can't fight a war if you don't know your enemy. Call it laziness or distraction, but we so often fail to name our opponents. If you can't name your opponent, you'll likely fight over it rather than go to battle together against it.

As we mentioned earlier, one of the first opponents that entered our marriage weighed eight pounds and challenged our marriage to the core. Not every opponent needs a negative label; an opponent is simply anything that threatens to disrupt marital intimacy and lead to disconnection.

What or who is your opponent right now? Write it down and ask your spouse to do the same. Then discuss it together. Is it finances? Deployment? Differing views on parenting and discipline? Sex? A new baby? A struggling child? A move to a new state? An addiction? A health issue? A new job or business?

Opponents come and go. As you face down your opponents, what matters most has less to do with the opponent and more to do with you—specifically, that your focus is on seeking to understand your spouse's story about the opponent and what's going on within his or her heart.

In those early years of parenting when I asked Josh why he never asked about my heart, I had no idea the number of opponents we faced at the time. I'm grateful he chose to fight for me instead of turning away from me. It was the beginning of our own healing journey from feeling like roommates to falling in love all over again.

That's because fighting together brings us together.

Call Out the Elephant in Your Marriage

When I told Josh he'd started our marriage on a foundation of lies, it was in lighthearted fun. However, I didn't realize that there actually was a subtle opponent lingering underneath the surface of our relationship—an opponent that appeared on the last night of our honeymoon but later ballooned into the proverbial elephant in the room when we failed to name it as an opponent.

Excited to cap off a beautiful first week together as a married couple, we chose to have dinner at a Mexican restaurant where we'd been staying in Riviera Maya. Up until this point, our week had been glorious. We rested. Snorkeled. Slept. Ate lots of food. And, as Josh likes to brag, we consummated our marriage.

I think it's interesting how easy it is—especially early on in relationships—for our minds to somehow equate physical intimacy and vulnerability to, "I now have your back in every area of life." It sure didn't take long for it to not feel that way to me.

On the last night of our honeymoon, while sitting in that lovely Mexican restaurant, we got into one of the worst arguments to date in our marriage. I was in tears. And who was our opponent, you might ask? Church. Yes, we fought about church. But it became about so much more than church. And that opponent lingered around our marriage for years because we didn't call it out, and because we didn't step into the heart of the other, which left us divided.

While we were dating, I had left my church family to attend the church where Josh was leading a ministry. Now married, I expected we would find a new church, one in which we could both serve together. But this expectation blindsided Josh. He had no desire to leave his church. As I sat there in tears on the last night of our honeymoon, I felt alone and unprotected by the man I had trusted to protect my heart.

There were reasons Josh didn't want to leave his church, but they had less to do with where God was leading him than they did his with own unrecognized wounds. At the time, his identity and significance were tied to pleasing others, especially authority figures. That's what took center stage. As a result, his shadows kept him more focused on what others thought of him than what was best for our marriage.

We continued to show up and attend church most Sundays, but neither one of us experienced any peace about it. Though it robbed us of feeling truly connected at a spiritual level, the status quo was more comfortable than taking the actions required to make a change. And that's how an opponent turns into an elephant.

As it is with most opponents, the issue wasn't the issue. We first had to learn to step into one another's stories—to call out the elephant and see it from the other's point of view. Our failure to do that, and our choice to sweep the issue under the rug, caused our opponent—church—to turn into an elephant that came waltzing into the living room of our marriage every few months. When it did, we'd fight about it and then let it walk out again. But each time it returned, the elephant got bigger and bigger.

Whatever the elephant in your marriage might be—that big issue you don't want to talk about—if you don't name it and call it out, it will only continue to grow bigger and bigger. Any one of your opponents could become an elephant if you avoid dealing with it. But whatever the opponent may be, it's not your spouse.

Talk about Your Dance

JOSH

Once you name your opponent and call out any elephants in your marriage, it's time to talk about your dance, the patterned and dysfunctional ways in which you interact with each other. We all dance in marriage in predictable ways. One of the things Christi and I learned, and something we coach couples to do, is to engage in metacommunication, which is communication about your communication. Again, the issue is not the issue. Instead, the issue is how you communicate about the issue in a way that champions the heart of your spouse. This includes paying attention to your tone of voice, the timing of conversations, eye contact, your use of "I" statements and avoiding the word "you" as a blame tactic, and even talking about how to best communicate your needs to each other.

Dr. David Burns has a list of ways we dance to self-protect. With a hint of sarcasm, I sometimes call these dance moves the dysfunctional ways we get our spouse to like us better by treating him or her like crap. See if you relate to any of these dance moves:

Sarcasm: expressing bitterness or ridicule with cutting words or tone of voice

Blame: putting the fault entirely on the other person

Self-blame: avoiding criticism or the other person's feelings by acting as if you're horrible or not good enough

Defensiveness: refusing to admit your own weaknesses

Passive-aggression: saying nothing about your feelings to the person's face but undermining the relationship by expressing those feelings indirectly

Problem-solving: trying to fix the issue while ignoring your spouse's feelings

Diversion: bringing up unrelated issues or changing the subject

Martyrdom: playing the victim

Labeling: name-calling

Counterattack: responding to criticism with criticism

Put-down: using hurtful words to belittle

Mind reading: expecting the other person to magically know how you feel

Denial: pretending the problem or your feelings about a problem don't exist

Hopelessness: insisting there's nothing else you can do[4]

We all have our dance. But when we fail to talk about our dance, we turn opponents into elephants. And the bigger the elephant gets, the more likely we are to make our spouse the enemy.

The dance Christi and I did in the early years of our marriage was a two-step back-and-forth between blame and defensiveness. If Christi was curt with me, I might protect myself with defensiveness (and a half-step of denial), refusing to admit any weakness or fault. I did this especially as it related to our issue with church. I was blinded by and ignorant of my wrongdoing. But I saw Christi's. I prioritized being right over guarding Christi's heart. And that became a bigger issue because, in so doing, I not only set Christi up to use her self-protective dance moves toward me but also set her up for negative comparison. I compared her to other wives who served alongside their husbands, and I selfishly wondered why Christi just couldn't join me in the ministry where I was already serving. Instead of listening to her heart, I was blinded by the insecurities I carried from my own story.

Setting up your spouse for negative comparison is the danger you face when you fail to take personal responsibility for your role in fighting opponents and guarding your spouse's heart. John Gottman and Nan Silver say this is how we begin to subtly betray our spouse.[5] Betrayal starts by secretly wishing your spouse would act differently or even be someone different. Betrayal is a seed of doubt, a sign that the enemy is twisting your view of who or what your opponent really is.

Becoming famous at home, on the other hand, happens when you become president of your spouse's fan club.

Cheering for your spouse's heart.

Championing your spouse's strengths.

Helping your spouse become the best version of himself or herself.

Becoming teammates.

Meeting in the same locker room.

And adopting an "us against the world" stance to take out your opponents.

Remember when you first started dating and you saw everything you had in common, no matter how trivial?

"Oh, my goodness, you like spaghetti? I love spaghetti too! We're sooo meant to be together!"

Young and in love, you were blinded to the negatives and focused only on the positives. Being famous at home requires rekindling the giddiness of those early years. Being twitterpated by the thought of being on the same team.

When we feel loved, we start to make positive comparisons rather than negative ones. As our emotional needs get met in the relationship, our number of pro-relationship thoughts increases. Researcher Dr. Caryl Rusbult found commitment to be "a gradual process in which the partners come to compare the relationship favorably to others with increasing frequency."[6]

But you must bring into the light the ways you dance. Instead of trying to get your spouse to love you by being a jerk, start listening to your spouse's heart, even if it feels uncomfortable. And be ready to share how you feel in your dance. You know how your spouse makes you feel—the ways he or she makes you want to lean in and the ways he or she pushes you away.

Don't wait for an argument to talk about your dance. Doing so gives your real enemy a foothold (Ephesians 4:27). Instead, start now. The more you can bring these feelings into the light, talking about them when your fight, flight, or freeze defenses are down, the more open you will be to your own tendencies, and the more aware you will become of how you can fight for each other's story.

Declare Your Love

Your spouse is not your enemy. Your spouse is your greatest teammate.

In the same letter Paul wrote to the church at Ephesus about not giving the devil a foothold with our anger, he also said not to "use foul or abusive language" and to "get rid of all bitterness, rage, anger, harsh words, and slander" (Ephesians 4:29, 31). Sounds a lot like the dysfunctional ways we try to get our spouse to like us better.

"Instead," Paul wrote, "be kind to each other, tenderhearted, forgiving one another, just as God through Christ has forgiven you" (Ephesians 4:32). And in case anyone was looking for loopholes, Paul also wrote, "Let *everything* you say be good and helpful, so that your words will be an encouragement to those who hear them" (Ephesians 4:29, emphasis added).

Did you catch that? Everything you say.

You can begin to act on that by voicing your pro-relationship thoughts aloud. Find what you love about your spouse, big and small, and declare it.

"There's nobody I'd rather do life with."

"I love the relationship you have with God."

"I never imagined having a spouse who loves our kids the way you do."

"Thanks for fighting for my heart by doing ____________ for me."

"I appreciate the way you champion my strengths."

"We crushed it today. How fun was that?"

"What you said was really difficult to hear, but I know you want me to be the best version of me I can be. Thanks for being committed to my growth."

You both have a story. Your willingness to listen to your spouse's story and be vulnerable with your own story will keep you fighting for—not against—each other.

Your spouse is your greatest teammate.

Go write your victory stories together.

8

WHO ARE YOU BECOMING?

Why Parenting Is the Wrong Term

JOSH

I thought I was emotionally mature. Then I had kids. The whining, the fighting, the lack of sleep, the constant "needing." It's a lot for my kids to put up with.

But in all seriousness, what a perfect recipe for exposing the worst parts of us humans.

You don't have to be a parent for more than five seconds to feel like a failure. When we surveyed more than seven hundred parents and asked them to name their greatest parenting struggles, "too busy," ranked first, but "feeling inadequate" ranked second. The shame and guilt that come with feeling like you're too busy or that you're not a good enough mom or dad can cripple you into believing that you don't have what it takes to raise great kids.

Yet, this couldn't be further from the truth.

God wired you with everything your children need to grow up

and be amazing humans. That's why being famous at home with our kids requires rethinking the definition of what it means to be a parent.

Take a look. The definition of parenting is "the activity of bringing up a child as a parent."[1]

Simple enough, right? But think about the activities we engage in as parents and the things we spend the most time worrying about. Getting our infant to sleep. Disciplining a toddler's temper tantrums. Managing the flailing swords, the intentionally knocked over blocks, and the name-calling of sibling rivalry. Teaching responsibility. Getting our kids to be kind, do their chores, respect authority, sit at the table, and have good attitudes. Setting limits on video games. Teaching them to be smart with smartphones and drive responsibly.

Notice who is the focus of all the activity of parenting—it's the child. "The activity of bringing up a child."

Let's consider this same dynamic within the marriage relationship for a moment. When has trying to change an undesirable behavior in your spouse actually worked? What tactic did you use?

At one point, Christi tried to change me from making everything about me. In my mind, I was giving everything I had to serving everyone else. Resorting to martyrdom (playing the victim) and hopelessness (insisting I tried everything I could to no avail) were my tactics. And the more Christi tried to fix me, the more accusatory she became. How did I respond? I made it about me. I had to defend my contributions at home while still trying to manage work and put food on the table. Didn't she recognize that?

Nope.

She was trying to change me. And I was trying to change her. Neither of us had the energy or the wherewithal to recognize what needed to happen first. We had to change ourselves.

Now, let's return to the children.

Who complains until they get dessert? Who begs to stay up at bedtime? Who whines when you turn off the TV?

Your children.

Why? Because if they could just change you, maybe they could get more ice cream, stay up later, and watch another show.

But attempts at changing another human only result in bigger battles and more fighting. That's at least part of the reason why the act of parenting can feel so overwhelming—because the focus is all about changing the child.

What I'm about to say doesn't mean you won't still have to engage in the basic activities of parenting. But I hope it does remove the pressure you put on yourself in those activities. You do not have the power to change another person, your child included. The only person you have the power to change is yourself. And this couldn't be truer than in the world of parenting. That's why we prefer to use the word *becoming* to describe the primary activity of parenting. It's one little word but it is also a massive paradigm shift that can set you free.

From Parenting to Becoming

The word *becoming* means "the process of coming to be something."[2] Or, in our definition, the process of coming to be a great human.

Why is *becoming* a better paradigm than parenting? Consider this statement from researcher and bestselling author Brené Brown: "Who we are and how we engage with the world are much stronger predictors of how our children will do than what we know about parenting."[3]

When I first read this statement in Brown's book *Daring Greatly*, I highlighted it fourteen times, dog-eared the page, and attached a sticky note to mark it. I was thunderstruck at the generational implications. Our children will become by-products of how we manage our own emotions, how we treat ourselves, and how we engage the world around us, including how we treat a barista, a coworker, our child's teacher, and especially their other parent. In short, our children *become* who we *are*.

Trying to learn parenting techniques as a means of changing a child is exhausting. I'm not saying parenting techniques are not important or that they don't have a place. But trying to change another human—especially through nagging, punishments and rewards, or any other form of behavior modification—puts all your energy into the other person and drains you. Not only that, it's also not nearly as effective as investing your energy in yourself.

Want proof?

In a double-blind study that analyzed two thousand parents against proven parenting skills, researchers Robert Epstein and Shannon L. Fox identified the top ten parenting skills that were most predictive of raising happy, healthy, and successful kids. They found that behavior management—rewarding positive behavior and punishing negative behavior—ranked seventh. In other words, the parenting skill many of us use most is pretty far down on the list of ten. Perhaps it's no surprise, then, that Epstein and Fox found behavior management to be a poor predictor of a child's happiness, health, and success, and found parents to have "scored relatively poorly on this area."[4]

As humans, we do a terrible job of trying to change another person's behavior.

Even if that other person is our child.

It turns out that the number one parenting skill was also one most parents are really good at—showing love and affection. Numbers two and three surprised even the parenting experts interviewed for the study. Are you ready for this?

Number two was a parent's ability to manage his or her own stress. Let that one sink in for a moment. Researchers found this skill to be the most poorly practiced among parents. Don't believe the lie that practicing self-care is selfish, especially when it's found to be one of the most important skills for raising great kids.

Number three was how parents treat one another, either as a spouse or as a coparent in a divorce situation. Notice that this parenting skill has nothing to do with a direct relationship with the child. In fact, of the ten parenting skills that get the outcomes parents desire most in their kids, the top three have little or nothing to do with a direct relationship with a child. Instead, they have everything to do with who the parents are and who they are becoming.

Take the number one skill, showing love and affection. When we go to a counselor, there's a reason he or she spends so much time asking us about our relationship with our parents. The quality of our relationship with our parents or primary caregiver is a kind of trampoline that launches us into the world of relationships as an adult.

Some of us had parents who changed the springs of their emotional well-being and kept the relational trampoline bouncy, welcoming our coming down when we needed comfort and catapulting us into the world when we felt confident again. They created an environment that demonstrated love and affection.

Others of us had parents who let their relational springs rust or had experienced no relational trampoline from which to launch into parenthood. They created an environment that lacked love and affection to some degree. Such an environment might take all kinds of forms, from depression to alcoholism, or legalism to abuse. Unfortunately, such dysfunctional environments tend to be passed down from one generation to the next. When we grow up in a family with generational cycles of dysfunction, it's much more difficult to learn how to show healthy love and affection.

That's why we believe the parenting skill of showing love and affection is first and foremost about our own becoming as individuals. Remember what the apostle John wrote about the source of love? "We love each other because he loved us first" (1 John 4:19). Our capacity to genuinely love another soul comes from our relational trampoline with God. And it was Jesus who said, "Love your neighbor as yourself" (Matthew 22:39). To love our neighbor requires that we first love ourselves.

Being loved precedes loving, just as becoming precedes parenting.

One of the primary conclusions of the study was, "All types of people are equally competent at child-rearing—and anyone can learn how to be a better parent with a little effort."[5]

"With a little effort."

Put another way: You become a better parent by becoming the adult you want your children to become.

I became a better parent when I started focusing on how I spoke to my kids even when I was stressed, how I greeted them each morning when they first saw me, and how I treated their mom when we disagreed. Do I always get it right? Of course not. But when my focus shifted from my kids' behaviors to my own, even my parenting activities changed. I got softer yet more confident in my discipline. I became more loving in my noes and more generous with my yeses. I even started picking up on more of what was happening in my children's inner worlds because I had learned new ways to quiet my own distracted inner world.

Again, becoming isn't about being perfect. Those who become famous at home put in the effort day in and day out behind the scenes. They become an overnight success a decade in the making because they don't see difficult days as steps back but as opportunities to show their kids how they're growing in perseverance, resilience, and self-awareness.

Your Story of Becoming

As you consider who you are becoming, it's helpful to have a counselor, coach, spiritual director, small group, or best friend help you. Don't fall into the trap of believing that counseling is for the weak-minded. The journey of discovering the broken fragments of your own story can be scary, but to invite someone along on that journey with you requires true courage.

In addition to therapy, your story of becoming might also include coaching. At Famous at Home, we see the most growth in coaching clients who employ both counseling and coaching. As a reminder, the focus in counseling is healing the brokenness of the past; the focus in coaching is working on the present and casting vision for the future.

As coaches, that's what we do—develop strategies that help couples and families find their direction and become famous at home in the process. And an essential part of that work, just as it was with Matt and Vanessa, is coaching spouses on how to enter into each other's stories first. If you're a solo parent, you can experience this by finding a small group, spiritual mentor, support group, or close friend who can enter your story and help you feel seen. It's important to have someone who listens to and helps you navigate the difficult parts of your story because it's the gateway to entering into your child's story.

When parents have trouble entering their child's or their spouse's story without overreacting, yelling, or jumping immediately to discipline (in the case of the child), it could be due to a blind spot in their own story. That's because a parent's instinct is to either parent the way their parents did or go to the opposite extreme because they didn't like the way their parents raised them. The problem in both cases is that the blind spot becomes a knee-jerk reaction, which means parents choose the way they parent without giving thought to it.

After coming to terms with some of my own blind spots, I began to filter my journey to becoming famous at home through the lens of one very important question: *What advice would I give to my children if they were faced with the same situation I'm in now?* This question alone often prompts me to reach out—to set up an appointment with my therapist, phone my pastor, or call a friend. The choices I make today reflect who my kids will become tomorrow. And I never want to be caught telling my kids to do something I was unwilling to do. Linking my parenting to my own story of becoming is what helps me to parent intentionally.

Having someone you can talk to about your own parenting tendencies provides a powerful mirror that reflects back to you the underlying motivations behind why you parent the way you do. Have you considered why you use the parenting techniques you use? Why you believe what you do about how you interact with your kids? Whether or not the parenting approach you use is getting the outcomes you want? If you are willing to engage such questions as part of navigating your own story, you will be in a much better position to enter your child's story without distractions and fears about how your children will turn out.

Your Child's Story

I'll never forget scrolling through Instagram one day and coming across a post by author Bob Goff: "Be the adult you needed when you were a child." Leave it to Bob to say in one sentence what took me an entire book to explain when I wrote *Safe House*.

Christi and I have a go-to parenting technique that stems from this idea. Before we do anything else in response to our children's behavior, we try to enter their story—whatever it is they're experiencing and feeling in that moment. This has been especially important with our daughter, Kennedy.

Kennedy is our "feeler." Because her older brother has such a bold personality, she developed a knack for storing up how she was feeling inside. When we first realized this, we couldn't tell if she was confused about whether she was allowed to share her feelings or if she just wasn't being given a chance.

So when we noticed that even the tiniest of inconveniences sometimes sent her into tears, it was a signal that she had been storing away some feelings. We started by asking whether she was hungry or tired. But sometimes she was feeling something deeper.

When she was disrespectful, our antennas went up even more. When she was blatantly disobedient, it was time to put on our see-through goggles to look into her heart.

If, because of distraction or busyness, we missed any cue that something was bothering Kennedy, her attitude came out like a roaring lion.

Why?

Because someone important in her life wasn't entering into her story.

And she was *feeling* it.

What do we do in moments such as these when our instinct, or everything we've been taught, is to discipline her into obedience? Do we send her alone to her room? Put her in the corner for a time-out? Take away privileges?

No.

We hold her.

Even in her defiance.

We hold our kids in our arms and let them cry. We give them permission to be angry. We don't lecture or say a word. We just embrace them.

Within minutes, we feel their little muscles begin to relax. Their personalities begin to resurface. Their minds begin to calm down.

Only when they relax can we teach. Only when their minds calm can we discipline behavior. And not until they reengage with us relationally can we problem-solve for a solution to whatever got them so upset in the first place. It's not that discipline doesn't matter or has no place. It's that applying it without first entering their story only serves to further isolate our kids from us relationally.

This verse deserves repeating: "Such love has no fear, because perfect love expels all fear. If we are afraid, it is for fear of punishment, and this shows that we have not fully experienced his perfect love" (1 John 4:18). I repeat it because the instinct for so many of us when our kids misbehave is to rush toward discipline and truth telling and to neglect preserving the relationship through grace-based listening.

Don't misunderstand. Just as God disciplines those he loves, we, too, must discipline our children. But when a child's mind is already overwhelmed with emotion, being quick to anger, fast to lecture, or swift to set a consequence will only serve to ratchet up the emotion, not calm the mind. When your children already feel alone, disciplining them out of your own parental fears or blind spots will feel more like punishment, not loving correction.

This is why your story of becoming precedes parenting.

The next time one of your children is overwhelmed, try to enter their story the way God himself fathers you. He sees your weakness, and he remembers that you are "only dust" (Psalm 103:14). He knows that you are utterly dependent on how he treats you.

The LORD is compassionate and merciful,
slow to get angry and filled with unfailing love.
He will not constantly accuse us,
nor remain angry forever.
He does not punish us for all our sins;
he does not deal harshly with us, as we deserve.
For his unfailing love toward those who fear him
is as great as the height of the heavens above the earth.
He has removed our sins as far from us
as the east is from the west.
The LORD is like a father to his children,
tender and compassionate to those who fear him.

PSALM 103:8–13

We can step into our child's story just as God steps into ours. If we don't, we run the risk of provoking our kids to anger in the way we treat them (Ephesians 6:4). And even though discipline is never enjoyable in the moment, the Bible says, "It pays off big-time, for it's the well-trained who find themselves mature in their relationship with God" (Hebrews 12:11, MSG).

I love this because the payoff of discipline is relational maturity. And it's our own maturity that leads to our kids' relational well-being.

Now that you've seen parenting through the new lens of becoming, what one parenting technique or strategy might you need to give up? What isn't working but has been hard to let go of? Why are you hanging on to that strategy? What fears do you have about what might happen if you give it up?

From the perspective of becoming, what do you want to change in how you relate to your kids? What do you need right now for your own becoming? Do you need a weekend away to experience the love of the Father? Or a marriage getaway to fill your love tanks so you can show up for each other as a unified front with the kids? Do you need to reach out to a counselor or coach to discover new ways to manage your own stress?

Give yourself permission to focus on your own story. Because who you are becoming matters for your child's story.

★

PART 3

SEVEN DECISIONS TO PUT YOUR FAMILY CENTER STAGE

JOSH

I'll never forget being out for a walk one afternoon with a friend of mine, a friend very famous to the world, who is the definition of a go-getter. He said, "Josh, in my circles, we want to be famous at home, but our profession is demanding. What are five to seven things we can apply today to be famous at home?"

His question and the discussion that followed is what led us to develop the Seven Decisions. These are not tips, steps, or ways to become famous at home. As I explained to my friend, it's not that easy. You have to make decisions every day about how you show up, decisions that flow first from your own self-awareness. You must be aware of how your identity is caught in the balance between the demands of the world and the little eyes looking up at you wondering if you'll be at their game. That's why we want you to first understand the deeper reasons why acting on these decisions may or may not come easily for you.

As you read through the Seven Decisions, you'll notice a progression from self-awareness to others-awareness, and then to living out a family purpose that is so much bigger than your family alone. If you're like most people we coach, the challenge you'll face is focusing on finding your family's purpose when your career or other day-to-day responsibilities already demand so much of your time, attention, and identity. That's why putting your family center stage focuses on being decisive in simple moments of your day.

You don't have to add anything crazy to your already busy schedule. Putting your family center stage isn't necessarily about how often you show up; what matters most is *how* you show up. The Seven Decisions are designed to do that by helping you develop a lifestyle of showing up for the biggest fans under your roof.

Consider keeping a pad of paper or a journal nearby as you

read. Each chapter includes coaching questions and exercises, and you'll need a place to write down your responses. Or, if you have access to a printer, you can look for our downloadable worksheets at famousathome.com/book. You can use the worksheets to take notes and to record your responses to the coaching exercises. Either way, be sure to engage the exercises for each of the Seven Decisions. When you're done, you'll have a family plan ready to implement!

9

DECISION 1: CHANGE YOUR MINDSET

How to Show Up as the Best Version of You

JOSH

As a former high school baseball player, I naturally wanted our firstborn son, Landon, to play baseball. So I put him in T-ball—when he was four years old. I also decided to coach the team. I couldn't figure out why nobody else wanted to do it. Little did I know I'd need a certification in herding cats to coach T-ball.

One of my favorite memories of that first season happened when I told Landon to play second base. He ran straight for the base and stood on it. "Landon, you're not allowed to stand on the base when you play the field," I said. "Only the runner stands on the base." In the bottom of that same inning when Landon got to bat, he hit the ball and went sprinting for first base. Naturally, the first baseman was standing on the base to catch the ball and tag him out. But when Landon reached the base, he shoved the first baseman off the bag, apparently telling him only he, the runner, was allowed to stand on it. I never did earn my cat-herding certification.

After a few seasons, I realized I had put Landon in T-ball more for my own sake than for his, so Christi and I decided to hang up his cleats until he showed interest. Shortly afterward, I was talking to another dad in our neighborhood and told him of our decision to stop playing T-ball. "Josh," he said, sounding concerned, "you may want to reconsider. If you pull him out now, he'll be so far behind by the time he's ten he won't be able to catch up to the other boys." His response was a telling reflection of our current cultural view of success and achievement, which essentially says, "Make sure you invest every cent, every minute, and every ounce of energy on your children being 'all in' (with whatever the activity is) from as early an age as possible, or they won't make it." In other words, if your kids aren't successful, they'll lose their identity.

If parents feel this kind of pressure today about their kids' activities—and how success is tied to their children's identity—imagine the trickle-down effect on the kids. Sports and activities are great for kids, but when the culture around you tells you that your kids need to be the best from the age of four, think carefully about what that means. Never-ending practices, private coaching sessions, and games that put undue pressure not just on your child but on every person in your family become commonplace. Phrases like "running ragged," "it never stops," and "not enough time" will play on repeat in your mind—and in your home. Meanwhile, the child involved in the activity will feel the stress, and the child(ren) not involved will feel dragged along for the ride.[1]

Guilt feeds on busyness and everyone going their separate ways. And though you might see one another at dinner here and there or in the morning as everyone leaves for the day, you'll feel more and more like you don't actually *see* one another. The relational and emotional distance grows. When you first notice it, you might disregard it as a fleeting thought. But the nagging sense that something feels amiss in your family won't leave you. You'll lie in bed at night wondering when life will slow down or worrying about the growing distance you feel in your marriage. Perhaps you already do.

When we succumb to the narratives of the culture around us, our lives start to look like the lives of everyone else in the culture. When busyness and success are cultural values, we'll find ourselves not having enough time for one another, let alone ourselves. Over time, the dissonance we feel between life as it is and life as we want it to be, or think it should be, widens. We become so entrenched in life as everyone around us is living it, we have no idea how to get from where we are to where we want to be because we know no other way of life.

There is another way. But the course correction you need to make for your family requires a fundamental shift of mindset—your mindset. While that may initially feel overwhelming, the good news is, it doesn't have to be. It *is* possible to change course.

Changing Course

Before pilots take off, they put together a flight plan to detail their planned route. And to get from one point to the next on their journey they "vector" by making a series of gradual turns toward their destination. They also rely on input from air traffic control to set or change their course based on headwinds, storms, air traffic, and other variables. Without that support, pilots might be forced to make a hard, ninety-degree turn to avoid an unforeseen storm. Instead, and fortunately for us as passengers, pilots can vector their turns a few degrees at a time over distance to safely reach their destination.

A similar principle applies when it comes to making Decision 1: Change Your Mindset. The routines and rhythms your family has developed didn't just happen. Your mindset and beliefs about how you do or don't do family life are complex and have likely developed over months and years. It's unrealistic to think you can make a ninety-degree turn by implementing big changes overnight—especially without outside support—and have them stick over time. Remember, becoming famous at home is a lifestyle change, one that happens gradually. And lifestyle changes require the kind of transformation that happens more like vectoring, by smaller degrees and at varying speeds over the course of distance and time.

The starting point for such incremental change begins with changing how we think. The apostle Paul wrote:

> Do not conform to the pattern of this world, but be transformed by the *renewing of your mind.* Then you will be able to test and approve what God's will is—his good, pleasing and perfect will.
>
> ROMANS 12:2, NIV, EMPHASIS ADDED

Based on our personal experience and the experiences of those we have the privilege of coaching, I feel confident in saying that 90 percent of the success and growth in your marriage and family comes down to renewing your mind.

Renewing your mind toward your identity.

Renewing your mind toward your spouse.

Renewing your mind toward your kids.

Renewing your mind toward your work.

Renewing your mind toward God's plan for your family. Yes, we believe he has a ridiculously cool plan for how he wants to use your family for his Kingdom!

Mindset is the single most important shift you can make to become famous at home. And even though you need support, no one can make that mindset shift but you. Because the only person you can change is you.

Even so, making the decision to change yourself might feel overwhelming, especially if you genuinely believe it is your spouse or kids who really need to change. With so many moving parts in your family, it's easy to think, *We have so many problems; where do we even start?*

Start with you.

Vector Your Mindset to a New Destination

CHRISTI

Changing your mindset is about identifying one aspect of your life that will help you show up better for your spouse and kids. Though it might feel like a monumental shift, your mindset changes when you vector your time, attention, and identity toward a new destination—showing up as the best version of you for your loved ones.

Start by identifying your greatest pain point, defining your first goal, and setting your first rhythm.

Identify Your Greatest Pain Point

The first question we ask prospective coaching clients is, "Why did you reach out to set up a call? What's your greatest pain point right now?"

Pain points can be anything that keeps us from showing up as the best version of ourselves for our loved ones. Pain points can also range from a nagging sensation that something feels "off" in your family relationships or the direction of your family as a whole, to a clanging alarm that everything is about to fall apart.

One way to identify your greatest pain point is to ask yourself what keeps you up at night. How would you complete the following statements?

What keeps me up at night is ____________.

Our lives would be so much better if we could just ____________.

Your answers are likely a signpost pointing to your greatest pain point.

Josh and I often hear pain points like these from coaching clients:

- "I feel like we're just roommates."
- "I keep missing my kids' events. I want to be there for them, but right now I just have to grind this out. Once I [get this business off the ground, get a promotion, finish this project], then I'll be able to show up and be at my kids' events."
- "I have such a desire to [start a small business, go back to school, plan an event, take our family on a trip], but by the time I put the kids down at the end of the day, I feel drained and unmotivated to do anything."
- "We haven't been together much as a family, but we know it's just a season and we're going to keep pressing through."

Another way to identify your greatest pain point is to consider the challenges your family is facing right now.

- Do you feel so disconnected from your spouse that you'll be heading for divorce if you don't do something soon?

- Do you miss too many special moments with your kids because your career, busyness, or other distractions pull you away from home?
- Are stress and lack of self-care preventing you from being truly present with those you love most?
- Do you feel alone or left behind, or do you resent your spouse because of his/her career?
- Do you feel your family's spiritual life takes a back seat to the demands of the world and individual achievement?
- Are members of your family being pulled in different directions with no unity or shared purpose?

Set aside some time to reflect on the challenges you and your spouse are facing right now. They might be physical, financial, relational, vocational, emotional, or spiritual struggles. Write down what you consider to be the three greatest pain points. Use the following prompts:

My greatest personal struggle is ______________________.

Our greatest marriage struggle is ______________________.

Our greatest parenting struggle is ______________________.

Once you both have identified your pain points, talk to each other about them. What similarities and differences do you notice in the struggles you identified? Are there any surprises? When recently have you experienced each pain point? After talking through your lists, narrow down the pain points to the heaviest one each of you is carrying individually right now. Here's the key question to ask:

Which of the three pain points is preventing you from showing up for your loved ones most? Or, which one, if alleviated, would help your family most? Is it your personal, marital, or parenting pain point? Which one is your spouse's biggest pain point?

As you approach this discussion, keep in mind that even talking about pain points can be difficult. In fact, sometimes our frustration, worry, shame, or feelings of inadequacy are too heavy to put into words, especially the first time we allow ourselves to admit what is heavy, where we lack joy, what we've lost, or how alone we feel.

All those years ago, I was completely surprised when Josh, after weeks of fighting his own internal battles, told me about the weight he was carrying and his fears of life getting out of control. Until he verbalized it, I didn't have a clue about how burdened he felt. Shame kept him enslaved to his pain.

The same was true for me. I often kept my struggles to myself. I didn't want to burden Josh since I knew he couldn't relate. When I finally had the courage to say my pain points aloud, not only did my burden feel lighter, I also gained an ally. Josh had no idea how my struggle as a mom was stealing so much joy from me, but once he did, he could help me get it back.

Though we can't always relate to our spouse's pain points, sharing them enables us to fight for each other. When we bring our pain points into the light, Josh and I become a team warring against an adversary who wants nothing more than for us to keep our pain, fear, and shame to ourselves.

Define Your First Goal

Once you identify your one greatest pain point, the next step in changing your mindset is to define your first goal. One goal—not five or six. You can't solve every problem overnight, nor should you try. It's okay to start small.

Your goal is one thing you can do to alleviate your greatest pain point so you can reach your destination—showing up as the best version of yourself for your family. Here are some examples:

- *I will prioritize reconnecting with my spouse and take the necessary steps to become a better husband/wife.*
- *I will show up for my kids by discovering what makes them feel loved and prioritized.*
- *I will implement a healthy diet, exercise, and/or a self-care plan so I can be the best version of myself for my family.*
- *I will invite my spouse to help me find out what brings me alive and gives me a sense of purpose.*
- *I will talk to my spouse about finding a faith community for our family.*
- *I will find a counselor or family coach to help our family live with intentionality and purpose.*

Now it's your turn. Based on your pain point, write your first goal. Don't overthink it. What outcome would alleviate your pain point? Write that.

My first goal: *I will* ______________________________.

Set Your First Rhythm

Once you define your first goal, you'll want to make it measurable and actionable by adding a new rhythm to your life. By rhythm, we mean a routine practice that will enable you to achieve your goal over time. Think of this as vectoring your lifestyle to reach your destination.

Being famous at home and living a healthy and holistic lifestyle—which includes your marriage, parenting, physical health, spiritual health, emotional health, financial health, and work ethic—lives and dies on the habits you develop and the rhythms you set. In the list of examples below, you'll notice that some are daily rhythms and others are weekly rhythms. Whether you practice your rhythm daily or weekly, the main thing is to choose a rhythm that enables you to achieve the goal of alleviating your pain point.

- *I will set up a weekly counseling/coaching session for us as a couple. If my spouse is unwilling to go with me, I will attend individual therapy to become a better spouse and version of myself.*
- *I will eat dinner with my kids every night and use FaceTime if I'm out of town for work.*
- *I will turn off my phone and play with the kids for twenty minutes a day.*
- *I will work out for thirty minutes four days a week.*
- *I will tell someone about how I self-medicate and implement a plan to quit (drinking alcohol, eating sugar, binge watching shows, etc.).*
- *I will make an appointment with a nutritionist to develop a healthy eating plan.*
- *I will turn off my phone for the first hour I'm awake and for the last hour before I go to bed.*
- *I will set aside two hours a day while the kids nap to launch my new business.*

- *I will commit an hour a day to starting a garden.*
- *I will meditate each morning for thirty minutes.*
- *I will visit and attend a new church weekly until we find a healthy faith community.*

What one new rhythm could you implement to make slow but steady progress toward your first goal? Make it measurable and actionable. And remember, the new rhythm is designed to help you show up as a better version of yourself for those whose character you have the privilege of getting to shape.

My first rhythm: *I will* ______________________.

You really can change your mindset. All it takes to change course is vectoring a few degrees over time by defining one goal and setting one rhythm to reach your new destination—showing up as the best version of yourself for your loved ones.

Why Your Rhythms Matter

JOSH

When the pandemic hit in 2020, I moved from speaking in person at events to speaking remotely via online webinars and livestream events. Being at an event in person is much easier. At home, my kids interrupt me quite a few times a day to ask what I'm doing, when I'll be done working, and if I can play with them. Though it's sweet, it can also be guilt inducing because I feel like I need to be with them when I'm home.

One pain point I had that year was feeling as if I was constantly saying no to my kids, because even though I was with them way more often throughout the day, I still had to work. I set a goal:

I will enter my kids' worlds more often throughout the day. My new rhythm: *I will say yes at least twice a day to their requests to play with them or enter their world.*

One day was exceptionally busy. I got up before the kids to write, spent the day doing corporate coaching, and had a livestream speaking event beginning at 6:00 p.m. Having already run a technology test with the event hosts, I sat waiting at my desk with my microphone on mute and video camera turned off. At 5:50 p.m., my sweet daughter, Kennedy, walked in, gave me a hug, and said, "Daddy, I didn't get to play with you today. Can we play Uno when you're done?"

I knew she'd be asleep before the event was finished. Having made the decision to change my mindset so I could be present with my kids, and knowing I had ten minutes to spare, I said, "No, honey, you'll be asleep before I'm done. But you know what? I missed playing with you today, too. Can we play right now for ten minutes before I speak?"

Her face lit up like a Christmas tree at the climax of a Hallmark movie.

We ran to the top of the stairs and played a few hands of Uno together before my talk. It was easily the best ten minutes of my day. The simple daily rhythm of saying yes changed my mindset. And my little girl's day!

A few years ago, when I first began implementing the Seven Decisions myself, I heard psychologist John Gottman suggest a question I carry with me to this day: "If your kids ask you to do something, ask yourself the question, 'Why not?'"[2] Why not read one more book before bed? Why not jump on the trampoline even after we've already had our showers for the day? Why not play Uno for ten minutes?

Kids hear us say no way more than they hear us say yes. And

many times, it's for no compelling reason. So why not say yes instead? I also started applying the question when Christi made requests, and even though I sometimes say yes to things I don't feel like doing, we have so many more good memories because of it. Ask yourself the question, "Why not?" and if you can't come up with a legitimate answer, say yes and let the memory unfold.

Saying yes to Kennedy in that moment wasn't easy. But I had enough self-awareness to know I could pull it off on my end and still make her night. The reason I say yes more often now—to both Christi and the kids—is because I learned that my default mindset of saying no had more to do with me than it did with whatever Christi or the kids were asking. I just needed to be aware of what was going on within me so I could change my mindset and step into the moment. Because to those under my roof, it really matters that I show up as the best version of me.

Matt and Vanessa's journey began in a similar way. Matt's first new rhythm was nothing fancy. He simply decided to pray for Vanessa and their kids every day. Not just a five-second, "Lord, bless my wife and kids today" prayer. He spent time every day praying specific prayers for each person and asking God to help him see his wife with the same love and affection God has for her. He first offered what he had to give.

After a week, he added another new rhythm. He didn't beat himself up for not doing more. He measured his progress against what he'd done the day before. You know what Vanessa's first rhythm was? To compliment Matt for taking one specific action each day. To notice him. To be kind to him.

Implementing their new rhythms shifted Matt and Vanessa's mindsets toward their biggest fans. When they took one small step to make a change, they began to show up for each other in new ways. Instead of resentment, Vanessa chose kindness. Instead of emotional disconnection, Matt chose spiritual engagement. When Matt and Vanessa followed through on their new rhythms, they changed their family.

As you establish one new rhythm to meet your first goal and follow through on it day after day, your mindset will begin to shift. Remember, you can't change anyone else in your home, but you can change your mind about how you show up.

Surround Yourself with Support

The toughest part of Decision 1 is taking responsibility for your new rhythms. And you'll greatly increase the odds of reaching your destination if you surround yourself with support. In other words, if you want to maintain your new rhythm, it really helps to have someone to answer to. For Matt, that was a men's group. For Vanessa, it was a spiritual mentor. Depending on your goal, that person could be your spouse. Solo parents, I know it's not easy, but make sure you ask for help. You have to fight for self-care more than any of us, and you deserve it. Don't be afraid to ask people in your inner circle for help.

You and your family will also need spiritual support. With virtually every couple we coach, we see things get worse before they get better. That's partially because couples have to have difficult conversations to tackle some of their opponents. But it's also because as families start finding freedom to be who God created them to be, the enemy ups the ante. Being famous at home is an eternal journey, not a temporal one. That requires growing spiritually as well as relationally. If your desire is to take your faith to a new level as a family, you *must* cover your family in prayer.

Find people you know who will commit to praying for you. Christi and I have a team of seven people we text when we need prayer. We do life with these people, and we know they are on their knees on our behalf when we're facing difficult times. Who are the prayer warriors in your circle? Invite them into your journey to keep you faithful to your rhythms when the enemy tempts you back into your old mindset.

Remember, you can't simply will yourself to change. The way you relate to your spouse was wired into your mindset over time. Changing that mindset won't happen overnight. But it can happen when you're willing to call out your pain point, set a goal, and establish a new rhythm—vectoring your lifestyle to become the best version of you for those you love. That's how you can rewire your mindset toward your loved ones and put them center stage. And one rhythm at a time, over time, will change the atmosphere of your home.

10

DECISION 2: CHANGE YOUR ATMOSPHERE

How to Cultivate a Life-Giving Environment

CHRISTI

Your home always has an atmosphere. And even in the most ordinary moments, the choices you make affect that atmosphere, sometimes for better and sometimes for worse. Consider the following three scenarios, each of which portrays the atmosphere in the Straub home on an ordinary morning.

Scenario 1: Exhaustion. I wake up looking forward to alone time before anyone else is out of bed but soon discover one of the kids is already awake. Before I've even brushed my teeth, it feels like the day is failing to meet my expectations. Feeling sorry for myself, I walk downstairs for coffee. Josh is already awake and oozing with overwhelm. With his mind in overdrive, he gives me a halfhearted "Good morning" before dropping the line I already knew was coming: "Is it okay if I leave early to get a head start on my work?" As he heads out the door, I start breakfast for the kids.

Scenario 2: Contentment. I wake in the morning and walk downstairs to peaceful worship music already playing in the living room. Josh had gotten up earlier to work out. As he comes in from the garage, he greets me with a kiss on the forehead. I grab my coffee, Bible, and journal, and settle contentedly in the living room. Not wanting to interrupt my alone time, Josh heads upstairs for a shower. When the kids come downstairs, they come by for a hug before going into their playroom to read a book together. I assure them we'll start breakfast in fifteen minutes.

Scenario 3: Joy. I wake in the morning looking forward to alone time but already hear "Momma" coming from Micah's room. I can't help but smile. Scooping him up, I hold him close and kiss his neck until he giggles. After changing his diaper, I carry him downstairs so I can make some coffee. As I turn the corner into the kitchen, Josh greets Micah and me with a warm smile. He opens his arms and pulls me in for a hug. "Good morning, love! How was your sleep?" As I settle Micah into his high chair, Josh pours me a cup of coffee and then we pray together for a few minutes. I feel so welcomed, even desired, as I begin my day. As the two older kids walk into the kitchen for breakfast, they snuggle up to Josh and me for a family hug.

Though the circumstances are similar in each of the three scenarios, the atmospheres the kids encounter when they come downstairs for breakfast are very different, ranging from exhaustion to contentment to joy. Just a few decisions make a big difference in how we all begin our day.

Decision 2 is Change Your Atmosphere because it only takes small shifts to dramatically turn the atmosphere of your home into a life-giving environment.

Understanding Your Atmosphere

So, what exactly do we mean by *atmosphere*? And how do we cultivate it and make it life-giving? The *Cambridge Dictionary* defines atmosphere as "the character, feeling, or mood of a place or situation."[1]

Think back to Matt and Vanessa at the beginning of their journey. The atmosphere of their marriage was disconnection and resentment, which was far from a life-giving environment for either one of them or for their kids. A simple change in Matt's rhythm began to shift the atmosphere toward engagement; a change in Vanessa's rhythm began to shift the atmosphere toward kindness. Although they both still felt a bit uncertain at first, the ongoing change in their mindsets steadily shifted the atmosphere over time, cultivating a more life-giving atmosphere of trust.

To help you assess the atmosphere of your home, we've compiled a list of the eleven atmospheres we often see in the couples we coach. We've placed each one on a continuum to show the negative and positive aspects of that atmosphere. We've also included a blank continuum at the end that you can use to assess an atmosphere unique to your home. On each continuum, circle the number that best describes the degree to which that atmosphere characterizes your home. Complete the assessment individually first and then review your responses together.

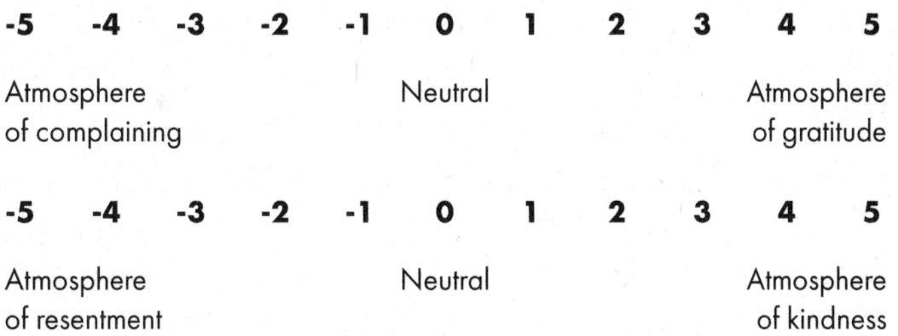

-5	-4	-3	-2	-1	0	1	2	3	4	5
Atmosphere of fear					Neutral					Atmosphere of peace

-5	-4	-3	-2	-1	0	1	2	3	4	5
Atmosphere of despair					Neutral					Atmosphere of hope

-5	-4	-3	-2	-1	0	1	2	3	4	5
Atmosphere of anger					Neutral					Atmosphere of patience

-5	-4	-3	-2	-1	0	1	2	3	4	5
Atmosphere of melancholy					Neutral					Atmosphere of joy

-5	-4	-3	-2	-1	0	1	2	3	4	5
Atmosphere of indifference					Neutral					Atmosphere of love

-5	-4	-3	-2	-1	0	1	2	3	4	5
Atmosphere of hostility					Neutral					Atmosphere of gentleness

-5	-4	-3	-2	-1	0	1	2	3	4	5
Atmosphere of entitlement					Neutral					Atmosphere of self-control

-5	-4	-3	-2	-1	0	1	2	3	4	5
Atmosphere of unreliability					Neutral					Atmosphere of trust

-5	-4	-3	-2	-1	0	1	2	3	4	5
Atmosphere of exhaustion					Neutral					Atmosphere of rest

-5	-4	-3	-2	-1	0	1	2	3	4	5
Atmosphere of _______					Neutral					Atmosphere of _______

Set aside some time to discuss your responses with each other. Which atmospheres, if any, did you assess as a negative 4 or 5? Which, if any, did you assess as a positive 4 or 5? Which two or three atmospheres would be most life-giving to you? What stands out to you about your assessments overall? After discussing your assessments, identify one atmosphere you'd like to change first—the one that would make your home and marriage more life-giving. What number are you at now in that atmosphere? Where would you like to be?

When you decide to change your atmosphere, remember that it's okay to start small. Instead of trying to change a negative 5 to a positive 5, aim to make a smaller shift. For example, from a negative 5 to a neutral 0 on the continuum. That's still a significant change. Remember, the goal is not dramatic and sudden change but steady and sustainable progress over time.

And here's some good news. The personal rhythms you set in Decision 1 should already be changing the atmosphere of your home. The more you change your mindset, the bigger influence you have on cultivating a life-giving atmosphere in your home. Rhythms change your mindset, and mindset changes your atmosphere.

In our work with families, we encourage couples to work on two kinds of atmospheric shifts—family shifts and supernatural shifts.

Family Shifts

There are three kinds of family shifts you can make: a personal shift (which is related to Decision 1), a marriage shift, and a kid shift.

Personal Shift

Your personal shift flows out of the rhythm you created in Decision 1. However, if you feel like your mindset shift isn't directly impacting the atmosphere of your home, you can add another personal shift to help cultivate a more life-giving environment. For example, one of the rhythms Josh uses to better show up for me and the kids is waking at 5:30 a.m. to work out. That definitely changes how he shows up for us throughout the day. Having taken time for himself, Josh is ready to help with the kids and greet all of us with a smile. Instead of starting the day with a begrudging attitude, worried about not having enough time to get things done, Josh begins with a full cup that spills over into ours. However, the atmosphere of our home at one time was actually impacted more directly by another of Josh's behaviors, which was his tendency to catastrophize.

He readily said things like, "What a disaster," or "There's no way that can happen," especially when he wasn't doing well. There's a heaviness to negative words, and there was a season in which I often found myself carrying the weight of Josh's words. For good reason too. The Bible says, "The tongue has the power of life and death" (Proverbs 18:21, NIV). So it only makes sense that the words we speak have a lot of power to change the atmosphere of our home.

Josh didn't believe me at first when I pointed out how often he used such phrases. But he agreed to make a personal shift—to speak life-giving words. Not long after, he caught himself using negative language more than he thought. Catastrophic language had become second nature to him. His choice to shift from an atmosphere of death to an atmosphere of life with his words changed everything—how we related to each other, the decisions we made, and how we ordered our days.

Is the rhythm you set in Decision 1 directly influencing the life-giving environment of your home? If not, is there another shift you can make that might bring more life inside your home for your spouse and kids?

Marriage Shift

The atmosphere of your marriage has the power to shape the environment of your entire home. For that reason, Matt and Vanessa chose to first make a marriage shift because they knew their marital satisfaction was the primary factor influencing how they showed up with their kids.

When Josh and I realized we often took one another for granted, we made a marriage shift by choosing to verbalize appreciation for the small things each of us did. The shift was profound. I finally felt seen in ways I had never felt in our marriage. Instead of overlooking me or withdrawing from me when I was having a bad day, Josh started to notice all the tasks that had previously gone unseen or were taken for granted. He expressed his gratitude for the thank-you notes I wrote on behalf of the family. He thanked me for putting meal plans together for the week and for buying presents for our kids to take to birthday parties. Celebrating the small ways we crushed it throughout the week didn't just change the atmosphere of our marriage, it changed the atmosphere of our home.

How is your marriage influencing the atmosphere of your home? What is one shift you can make in your marriage to create a better atmosphere for your children?

Kid Shift

Let's be honest, kids can change the environment of the home in some not-so-life-giving ways. Bickering. Complaining. Crying. Repeat. Although their childish behavior doesn't give us permission to respond in kind, that's often what happens. We, too, act childish, and the result is a change in the atmosphere of our home. With the kid shift, we focus on how the kids are influencing us as adults and the overall environment, and we make the necessary shift to set a better example.

With young kids, the level of grumbling and complaining—about unloading the dishwasher, putting on shoes, making beds, wearing underwear—can be exhausting. My natural response is to get frustrated. And when I do that, nobody feels connected.

In the spirit of the apostle Paul's admonition, "Do everything without complaining or arguing" (Philippians 2:14), we chose to come together as a family and make a kid shift by setting a rule: We won't grumble or complain. To make this practical, we set out a complaint jar. Every time we catch our kids complaining, they have to put a quarter from their piggy bank into the jar. When Josh or I complain, we have to put a dollar in the jar. We began by giving our kids a chance to earn their money back with gratitude and good behavior. But now we choose to donate the money to a worthy cause instead.

How are your kids influencing the environment of your home right now? What shift can you make with your kids to bring about a life-giving environment and move toward the positive numbers on the atmospheric continuums?

Now that you've seen some examples from our family, what three shifts could you make right now to change the atmosphere of your home to be a more life-giving environment? If it feels overwhelming to implement all three at once, start with the one you believe will make the biggest difference for everyone in the home.

Personal shift: *I will* ______________________.

Marriage shift: *We will* ______________________.

Kid shift: *We will* ______________________.

Supernatural Shifts

In addition to the three family shifts, there are three supernatural shifts we encourage our coaching clients to make because of how effective they are in radically changing the atmosphere of the home. I wholeheartedly believe these shifts are supernatural because they invite God's presence into our environment. The three supernatural shifts are blessing, prayer, and righteousness.

The Shift of Blessing

When Matt and Vanessa first received marriage coaching, one of the most powerful insights for Matt was discovering how his tendency to withdraw created an atmosphere that made Vanessa feel unsafe in their marriage.

"It was during one of our first meetings with you guys," Matt recalled. "Vanessa looked at me and said, 'I don't feel safe.' I didn't get it until we talked through what she was actually feeling."

Vanessa's turning point was when Matt "got it" in that moment. "I remember him looking at me and saying, 'I. Love. You. No. Matter. What,'" she said. "That was the moment I knew, no matter what feelings we had, what difficulties we went through, he was fighting for me. That's what I needed."

In that moment, Matt and Vanessa made the shift to becoming each other's biggest fans. They chose to bless rather than criticize.

Creating an atmosphere of supporting each other and being united in spirit changed the trajectory of their marriage. Although they didn't know it at the time, it also helped prepare them for some challenges they were about to face as a family. (More about that later.)

One of the simplest ways you can become your spouse's biggest fan is to fully support the personal goal and rhythm they chose to implement in Decision 1. Even though your spouse's goal might not initially make sense to you—because they may be in a very different place than you—choose to bless your spouse in that goal. Instead of lamenting that they aren't doing the goal you want them to be doing, come alongside your spouse to bless the decision they have made and offer to help.

When Josh and I first started practicing the Seven Decisions several years ago, my first goal was to take care of my body. I had neglected my body and was paying a price for it. Among other things, I was suffering adrenal fatigue and back pain, and the ongoing deterioration of my body added insult to injury. As a result, I ate to comfort myself.

But imagine how I might have responded if Josh had made comments about me putting on weight or if he'd tried to get me to eat less. How do you think that would have gone over? Josh is wise enough to know when to keep his mouth shut. But he'll also be the first to admit that when I don't focus on my health, everyone else in the house feels it. The atmosphere of our home changes when I don't take care of my body. I feel insecure and get down on myself, and when I'm beating myself up, that tends to spill out in how I treat everyone else too.

So, even though it might seem like a small change, my first rhythm was to stop eating sugar. As part of that, I invited Josh to help hold me accountable—to be my biggest fan. Accountability didn't mean that Josh could now say anything he wanted about my eating habits. I needed to be objective and clear about the questions he was allowed to ask. Setting a black-and-white no-sugar policy was an easy accountability. If I chose to eat sugar, Josh had my permission to call me on it. And though we both wanted me further along than the goal of not eating sugar, it was that first rhythm that led to years of goal-making and healing for me. Over time, I embraced an entirely new nutrition regimen, met with a pelvic floor specialist, and worked with a physiotherapist to strengthen my back.

When Josh and I set our first goals and rhythms, neither of us focused on our marriage per se. But championing each other in our individual rhythms enabled us, over time, to show up as the best versions of ourselves in our marriage.

The rhythms Matt and Vanessa chose were focused on strengthening their marriage. Matt no longer withdrew as he had been doing, and that enabled Vanessa to feel safe again. And that was just the beginning of Matt and Vanessa's transformation story.

When you become your spouse's biggest fan, it changes the atmosphere of your home. Blessing is always safer and more powerful than criticism.

The Shift of Prayer

JOSH

For a long time, Christi and I didn't pray together. I figured our individual prayers for each other were enough. I also felt like a failure at times because I hadn't prayed much with her. But such justifications are precisely what the enemy wants because they lead to complacency.

So, today, if you called me for marriage help, one of the first things I'd ask you to do is to pray for your spouse every day, asking

God to show you how he views your spouse. Then pray for your spouse's needs through the lens of God's love for him or her. This leads to an immediate shift in mindset because even if you're being treated unfairly, you can begin to develop an understanding from a different vantage point about why your spouse might be so defensive.

Christi and I continue to learn how to pray for each other and our family. Instead of avoiding prayer in the hopes that "everything will work itself out," prayer is our immediate go-to. When something feels off, we fall to our knees in our home office, hold each other on the couch, or pray in a parking lot if we're traveling. When the going gets tough, we pray in the moment, trusting in Jesus' promise that, "If two of you agree here on earth concerning anything you ask, my Father in heaven will do it for you" (Matthew 18:19). Those are some powerful words.

When our son Landon went through a very difficult time at school a few years ago, we did all we could as parents, but something still felt off. When you have that off feeling, pay attention to it. After tucking Landon into bed one night, I got on my knees outside his bedroom door and prayed a prayer to renounce a spirit of fear. The very next day, we received a phone call from Landon's teacher. An out-of-the-ordinary situation had happened that morning at school that exposed the root of the fear. Had I not prayed, I believe I would have allowed that spirit of fear access to our home, continuing to make things feel off. As the one primarily responsible for the atmosphere of our home, I pay careful attention to when things don't seem quite right. And I stay on top of it by meeting with the Father.

Shifting the atmosphere of your home unequivocally happens when you pray.

The Shift of Righteousness

The shift of righteousness is another game changer for families. When we make Jesus our Lord, we gain right standing with God (Romans 3:22). In other words, we "become the righteousness of God" (2 Corinthians 5:21, CSB). Once we are made right, we change the atmosphere in our homes when we commit to living a life of holiness or being "set apart."[2] To be holy or righteous is to be different from the world.

The Bible makes some amazing promises about righteousness. Living in righteousness brings peace: "And this righteousness will bring peace. Yes, it will bring quietness and confidence forever" (Isaiah 32:17). Righteousness provides spiritual protection: "He is a shield to those who walk with integrity" (Proverbs 2:7). Righteousness makes our prayers powerful: "The earnest prayer of a righteous person has great power and produces wonderful results" (James 5:16).

The shift of righteousness is not so much about legalism or sin management. Instead, it's about choosing to live in God's presence. We want to be in God's presence. We want our kids to experience God's presence. And we want God's presence to go before us and lead our family. To seek his presence, we do our best to follow God's command: "You must be holy because I am holy" (1 Peter 1:16). For us, to be holy is to do what honors God.

We choose to live in God's presence when we are intentional about the music we listen to, the movies we watch, and the amount of time we're on social media. We choose to live in God's presence when we treat one another with gratitude and kindness instead of criticism and contempt. We choose to live in God's presence when we prioritize time in his Word, getting to know him better, and joining with him in how we love others.

Think about the influence of your prayers reaching God's ears.

If you walk with Jesus, you have the authority in his name to call on his presence and shift the atmosphere of your home. In the course of our work, we have clients who have literally seen angels protect their families firsthand. I'm not saying this will happen to you or that if you don't make these shifts God's presence won't be with you. What I am saying is that we see God show up in some remarkable ways for families who choose to make these supernatural shifts by becoming their spouse's biggest fan, praying together, and living righteously before him.

If we were coaching you personally, we'd encourage you to start with *one* atmospheric shift you need to make. As you consider both the family and supernatural shifts, which one would make the biggest difference for everyone in your home? What one shift would move you to positive numbers on the atmospheric continuums?

Make that shift today.

11

DECISION 3: TALK ABOUT EMOTIONS

How Emotional Safety Cultivates a Healthy Home

JOSH

A few years ago, the Joint Special Operations Command (JSOC) invited me to speak on the topic of emotional safety at their Force and Family Symposium. Imagine speaking on emotional safety to a roomful of men and women who spend their days training to capture or kill enemies.

I was quite intimidated.

Fortunately, it went well. I continue to provide regular training for the military on the topic of emotional intelligence and cultivating an emotionally safe environment. Why emotional safety? Because the very thing these men and women are trained to turn off to survive on the battlefield (emotions) is also the very thing they need to turn back on to survive when they return home.

Emotional intelligence (EQ) is crucial to being famous at home and putting your family center stage. The two foundational skills of emotional intelligence—knowing how you feel and why you feel the way you do (self-awareness) and knowing what another person is feeling and why he/she is feeling that way (others-awareness)—cannot be developed without identifying emotions. The more self-aware I am, the greater is my ability to show up and be truly present for others without making their pain or emotional state about me. The more others-aware I am, the more empathetic I can be. That's why Decision 3 is Talk about Emotions. You need everyone in your home to be comfortable identifying their emotions and fluent in describing what's happening in their inner world.

Emotional awareness is what helps you consider and draw out the underlying motivation behind the actions of another. It's what enables you to avoid the cancer of an affair or relational scandal. And it's what helps you to become an empathetic spouse and a more emotionally present parent. The problem for so many of us, even as adults, is how our unprocessed or unrecognized feelings wreak havoc on how we show up with others. King Solomon may well have been commenting about the power of emotions in leadership when he wrote, "Patience is better than power, and controlling one's emotions, than capturing a city" (Proverbs 16:32, CSB). So many people fail to capture their cities because they fail to first capture themselves.

The more you recognize emotions in all areas of your life, the more freedom you have to show up as your authentic self, rather than faking your way through the day or overreacting to others. Knowing yourself brings to conscious awareness the impact you have on those around you. And the more aware you become, the easier it is to help your loved ones feel safe in their most overwhelmed moments.

The first two decisions—Change Your Mindset and Change Your Atmosphere—help you to pay attention to your own inner world. Decision 3: Talk about Emotions helps you start paying attention to and empathizing with what's going on in the inner worlds of your loved ones. And believe it or not, understanding their emotions starts with understanding the brain. That's because talking about emotions creates neurobiological connections that lead to deeper intimacy.

How the Brain Grows

To understand the why behind talking about your emotions, it's important to first know some basics about how the human brain grows.

The brain grows from bottom to top, and from right to left.[1]

First, from bottom to top.

Bottom to Top

Your amygdala sits at the bottom part of your brain at the back of your head, where the brain meets the spinal cord. You may have heard the amygdala referred to as the center of our fight, flight, or freeze response. It's the primitive part of the brain, which means it houses our most instinctual, God-given response to fear or danger. We either *fight* the threat, take *flight* from the situation, or *freeze* in the moment.[2] When the amygdala is activated, you don't have to think to act. Your instincts take over to act or react with fight, flight, or freeze. This instinct is present from birth.

The top part of the brain, located behind your eyes, is known as the prefrontal cortex. It is responsible for the highest levels of brain functioning, which include but are not limited to emotion regulation, cognitive flexibility, language processing, social skills, problem-solving, and self-control. Utilizing this part of the brain requires our conscious thought and attention.

When life is going well, we tend to relate well to those around us. But when we encounter situations that create stress, fear, or pressure, our true relational style reveals itself. That's when the amygdala is triggered, which means we will likely respond in one of two ways. If we can consciously regulate emotion and maintain self-control, we will problem-solve and do our best to serve the relationships and the situation at hand. If we lack that ability, we will be hijacked by our emotions and potentially do damage to our relationships and the situation by reacting instinctively in fight, flight, or freeze mode.

Neuroscientists suggest that our prefrontal cortex doesn't fully develop until we're in our mid-twenties. However, when we as parents show up for our kids in overwhelming or fearful moments, we help cultivate the higher functioning parts of our kids' brains because we teach them to regulate their fear and connect in relationship.[3] As neuroscientist Daniel Seigel explains, the goal in parenting is to help our kids build a "window of tolerance," spending less time living from fear reactions and more time living in healthy interaction—connecting, playing, and learning—triggering the top part of the brain.[4] As adults, building this window of tolerance in ourselves is part of our own becoming.

When I wrote *Safe House*, Christi came up with a great phrase to sum up the power of emotional safety for our kids. She said, "Basically, what you're saying is, parenting isn't rocket science, it's just brain surgery." She was right. As parents, we help wire our kids' brains by how we show up for them in their most emotionally vulnerable moments.

Right to Left

The brain also grows from right to left. The right side of the brain is the experiential, here-and-now part of the brain—what we feel and experience in the moment. The left side of the brain is the linguistic, language processing side—where we put words to what we experience. There is also a middle part of the brain, which is called the corpus callosum, or what I like to call "the binding of the book."

When both sides of the brain are triggered simultaneously, they collaborate to create something like a story of what we're experiencing. The left brain puts words to our experiences, and the right brain tells us how we feel about what's happening. Together, they write a book on a given experience, taking fragmented pieces of our story and assembling them into a coherent narrative, which gives meaning to our moments. If we were to read only the right-side pages of this book, it would feel fragmented and not make a lot of sense. But the middle part of the brain—the binding of the book—holds both sides together and gives meaning to the entire story.

Take a moment right now to recall one of your most meaningful childhood memories. If we could sit together and you shared the memory with me, I'm certain you'd tell me your story with all kinds of sensory details. Like the childhood memories I have of Me-maw's house, this moment of yours is one I'm sure you've talked about countless times, replayed in your head, and felt at a deep level. We remember these parts of our story, both good and bad, more than others because our brain has used all its working parts to integrate the experiences into a coherent narrative. We think (left side), feel (right side), and relate (engaging the amygdala if fearful or stressed, and the prefrontal cortex to problem-solve and connect) all at the same time in these moments.

Being famous at home requires putting emotional language to our own fragmented stories. This is part of the process of becoming. If we don't experience this in childhood, we can do so in adulthood by finding a therapist, coach, pastor, small group, friend, or mentor who listens to our story, is comfortable with our uncomfortable emotions, and values our experience. This is how we begin to make meaning of and reframe the broken parts of our story.

This process is crucial because it enables us to be emotionally safe for our spouse and kids in their emotionally overwhelmed, fearful, and stressful moments. The more comfortable we become talking about emotions with our loved ones—without taking offense or defaulting to our own fear response—the better equipped we'll be to help them calm their fear responses and engage the higher functioning parts of the brain to regulate emotion and connect.

This is why everything we do at Famous at Home is rooted in emotional safety and emotional intelligence. A child who learns to verbalize and make sense of her emotions in an emotionally safe environment can calm her own fears and therefore access the highest functioning parts of her brain in the prefrontal cortex. And it's these cognitive skills—emotion regulation, language processing, cognitive flexibility, problem-solving, and self-control—that lead to every major outcome we desire in our kids.[5]

Why the Apostle Paul Could Have Been a Neuroscientist

Our oldest son, Landon, was born with a strong will. He challenged us a lot, especially in his toddler and preschool years. One such occasion happened while I was out of town speaking at an event.

When I called home to check in on Christi and the kids, Christi said, "Landon's in boot camp."

"What do you mean he's in boot camp?" I asked, concerned but with a hint of criticism in my voice.

"He won't listen," she said. "And I need you to help me discipline him."

The accusatory tone was evident. The story I was telling myself—and I'm pretty sure it's the story Christi was trying to convey—was that Landon was acting out, Christi was exasperated, and it was all my fault because I was too lenient.

Since I'm certain we're not the only ones who argue over parenting styles, let me explain the power of talking about emotions by using this parenting scenario and what the apostle Paul wrote to the Philippian church about how to use emotional intelligence in relationships.

In his letter to the church at Philippi, Paul wrote,

> Let your gentleness be evident to all. The Lord is near. Do not be anxious about anything, but in every situation, by prayer and petition, with thanksgiving, present your requests to God. And the peace of God, which transcends all understanding, will guard your hearts and your minds in Christ Jesus.
>
> PHILIPPIANS 4:5–7, NIV

Now, keep in mind that Paul was in prison when he wrote this letter. Not exactly a place known for emotional safety. Yet, he identified a few key principles that fall right in line with what we know about the neurobiology of the brain and relationships.

First, the Greek word translated as "gentleness" is *epieikeia*, and it conveys the idea of "forbearance" and "sweet reasonableness."[6] When we live from an atmosphere of joy, we exhibit sweet reasonableness in how we respond to everyone, especially at home when our spouse and kids are in a tense fight, flight, or freeze situation. To have forbearance is to show self-control, putting our temper and defensiveness in its proper place.[7] A synonym for the word *gentle* is meek, a quality Jesus highlighted in his teaching of the Beatitudes (Matthew 5:5, NIV). A meek person's reaction toward another reflects inward humility "founded in self-control."[8]

In other words, when you live in gentleness, you can better tolerate the criticisms, frustrations, and provocations of your loved ones because you recognize God's gentleness with your own complaints. Which means you recognize God doesn't wield his power over you to hurt you. And in the same way, you don't wield your power over your spouse and kids for your own self-interest.

I know what pushes Christi's buttons—the words to use, the tone of voice, and how to exploit her weaknesses. If I wanted to get anywhere with Christi when she told me Landon was in bootcamp on that phone call, I needed to be gentle, to bring my own emotions under control and empathize with her exhaustion. But that's not easy when you're the one put to the test because your fight, flight, or freeze response (the bottom part of the brain) has been triggered.

After commenting on gentleness, Paul then counseled his readers to be anxious for nothing. Instead of being anxious, he said they should pray. If I were to put his words in neurobiological terms, it might look like this: "Because the Lord is near, use your left brain to verbalize your fears and emotions—which you're experiencing in the here-and-now with your right brain—to God in prayer. When you do this, God will help reframe the meaning of what you're going through, his Spirit calming your overwhelmed mind and giving you peace."

Paul's counsel reflected good neurobiology as well as sound spiritual practice because he asked us to present our emotional requests to the Father "with thanksgiving." This is why we encourage everyone we coach to keep a gratitude journal—because thanksgiving changes our perspective, helping us to focus not on the emotional overwhelm of the circumstances, but on the God who is always with us in those circumstances.

When you talk about your emotions to God in an atmosphere

of gratitude, the peace of God guards your heart and your mind in Christ Jesus. And this isn't just any peace; this peace transcends all understanding. Even in what may feel like the worst of circumstances in your marriage, career, or family life, when peace makes no sense at all, Paul told us to talk about it with God, our emotionally safe Father who is with us to calm our fight, flight, or freeze response long enough so we can think straight again.

Paul then continued:

> Finally, brothers and sisters, whatever is true, whatever is noble, whatever is right, whatever is pure, whatever is lovely, whatever is admirable—if anything is excellent or praiseworthy—*think* about such things.
>
> PHILIPPIANS 4:8, NIV, EMPHASIS ADDED

Paul didn't tell us to think first and then be anxious for nothing. Instead, I suspect he understood that when we are anxious or overwhelmed or feel defensive, we can't think straight. So, his instructions were to first deal with our anxiety and then to focus our thinking on better things. As a crisis response trainer, one of the first things I tell people who are in crisis is, "Don't sell your house, don't leave your spouse, don't quit your job. Don't make any major decisions." Why? Because a person in crisis quite literally—at the neurobiological level—can't think straight.

Do you think praiseworthy thoughts toward your kids when they act out? Of course not. But our kids act out for a reason, and what they need in those moments is not our fight, flight, or freeze reaction, but our gentleness—our power under control—in their overwhelm.

Was I thinking anything noble, pure, lovely, admirable, excellent, or praiseworthy when Christi accused me of being too lenient with Landon? Absolutely not. I had to bring my power under control and first be willing to understand where she felt left alone as a parent. Verbalizing my own feelings of rejection and confusion helped Christi realize we were on the same team more than we had given each other credit for. But we couldn't talk about a strategy to deal with Landon without first talking about the emotions we felt toward each other in that moment. Though we didn't resolve the problem on the call, our gentler attitudes put us back on the same team and helped us both to show up and be more present—Christi with the kids at home and me at the event—until we came back together again.

Just as our heavenly Father gives us divine peace to calm our weary minds in overwhelming situations, we, too, in a finite way, can impart peace to calm the weary minds of our spouse and children when they find themselves in overwhelming situations. But doing so requires that we first get comfortable talking about emotions.

How to Make Your Home Safe for Talking about Emotions

When you suppress emotions, they control you. When you act impulsively on your emotions, they control you. When you distract yourself from your emotions, they control you. To take control of your emotions and put your family center stage, you have to make your home safe for emotions.

Start by taking an honest inventory of the emotional climate you grew up in. Use a journal or the downloadable worksheet to write down your responses to the following questions.

- When you were growing up, to what degree were you allowed to use "feeling words" (such as *angry, sad, afraid*)? What did you learn about expressing your emotions as a result?

- What is one message you learned about emotions in childhood that influences your marriage today—for better or worse?
- What is one message you learned about emotions in childhood that influences how you parent today?

Invite your spouse and kids to give you feedback. Ask your spouse:

- How do I show up for you in a way that makes you feel emotionally safe with me?
- When do you feel emotionally unsafe with me?

Ask each child:

- How do I show up for you in a way that makes you feel like you can share your emotions with me?
- What do I do that makes you want to shut down or feel like you can't share your emotions with me?

These humbling but powerful questions give us insight into our own levels of comfort and awareness in talking about our emotions and allowing room for others to share theirs.

The Power of a Feelings Chart

CHRISTI

To calm our brains is to put language (left side of the brain) to what we're experiencing in the moment (right side of the brain). One of the most helpful ways of learning to recognize and put language to your emotions is with a feelings chart. Some families already have a habit of discussing the day's highs and lows at the dinner table, but it's rare for families to create space for using feeling words to talk about the emotions experienced each day:

> "I felt *embarrassed* when I dropped my books at school today."
>
> "I felt *jealous* when I saw Mary's beautiful vacation with other friends on social media."
>
> "I felt *disappointed* when I saw my final test scores."

Use the feelings chart on page 147 to help you begin identifying your emotions and building your emotional vocabulary. The chart is organized around six primary emotions: joy, anger, disgust, fear, sadness, surprise. Listed under each category are words describing various accompanying feelings. That's because emotions and feelings are not the same. For example, pain, hunger, and exhaustion are feelings but not emotions. Whereas you can find a never-ending list of feelings, researchers contend that there are only five to eight universal emotions.

Your emotions reside in the limbic system, which is the most primitive and instinctual part of the brain. These God-given emotions are powerful and help you survive the world around you. Emotions help you recognize when something or someone is threatening, and they help you respond to danger. In other words, they help you act quickly to survive by signaling to you when something *feels* off.

From these emotions we experience all kinds of feelings—some are so intense we experience them physically. Others are so mild we dismiss or don't pay attention to them. But paying attention to what we're feeling is important. The challenge comes when we aren't sure how to recognize or describe what it is we're feeling. We

FEELINGS CHART

Common Feelings to Help Us Recognize Our Emotions

JOY
Alive
Brave
Calm
Cheerful
Confident
Content
Cooperative
Creative
Curious
Daring
Elated
Encouraged
Excited
Fascinated
Feisty
Focused
Glad
Grateful
Happy
Heroic
Hopeful
Humble
Independent
Loving
Optimistic
Peaceful
Proud
Relaxed
Secure
Silly
Sincere
Zealous

ANGER
Annoyed
Cruel
Embarrassed
Enraged
Envious
Frustrated
Furious
Grumpy
Impatient
Insecure
Irritated
Jealous
Offended
Resentful

SADNESS
Alone
Apathetic
Ashamed
Bored
Depressed
Disappointed
Discouraged
Distant
Distressed
Guilty
Heartbroken
Helpless
Hopeless
Lonely
Pessimistic
Quiet
Tired
Upset
Weary
Worthless

FEAR
Afraid
Anxious
Cautious
Concerned
Doubtful
Nervous
Overwhelmed
Scared
Shy
Suspicious
Terrified
Threatened
Timid
Uncertain
Worried

DISGUST
Awful
Despised
Disapproving
Gross
Hesitant
Judgmental
Sickened

SURPRISE
Astonished
Confused
Perplexed
Startled
Shocked

don't know if we're discouraged or tired, nervous or insecure, jealous or threatened. That's when it's helpful to use the feelings chart.

Feel free to print multiple copies of the feelings chart from the downloadable worksheets. Post a copy on your refrigerator or set a copy on your dresser or coffee table—anyplace you will see it often. Refer to it to increase your emotional vocabulary and to identify your feelings throughout the day.

If you have a young child, you might be interested in a children's book we wrote called *What Am I Feeling?*, which has an accompanying poster-sized feelings chart that uses images instead of words. You can pull out the perforated poster in the back and hang it in your child's bedroom. Whether you create space during drive time, dinnertime, or bedtime, help your kids learn to identify feelings each day with simple "I felt" or "I feel" statements. Using a feelings chart can teach your kids how to recognize when something feels off in relationships, give you insight into your kids' defiant behavior, and teach your kids empathy. One night, our feelings chart did all three.

I'll never forget the day Kennedy, our sweet little girl, was the defiant one. She copped such an attitude. I followed my parental instinct to resort to discipline, but nothing I did changed her attitude.

I was confused about her behavior, but by the time bedtime rolled around, I'd slowed down enough to show some "sweet reasonableness." I asked Kennedy to pull out her *What Am I Feeling?* book and point to what she was feeling. She pointed to the "angry" face.

"Is there another feeling you have right now?" I asked.

After she took a second to think, her little finger slowly made its way to the illustration for "sad." Then quickly to "embarrassed."

"Honey, did something embarrassing happen to you today?" I asked.

"When I was at Emma's house, she and Kinley wanted to just have playtime by themselves, and they went into Emma's room and locked me out."

The tears began to flow.

Empathizing with her feelings of rejection, I reached out and held her. The feelings chart enabled Kennedy to put language to her story. My gentle presence created a safe place in which she could calm her brain enough to tell me what she was feeling. Then we could problem-solve together to help her know what to do if something like that were to happen again.

Helping your son or daughter use a feelings chart to talk about their emotions not only helps you to see deeper into their inner world, it also gives you an opportunity to help your child develop empathy for others. For the same reason, early in Josh's career, he gave every court-referred juvenile he counseled a feelings chart in their first session. You cannot get a troubled young person to feel remorse for wrongdoing—which is an expression of empathy—if he or she was never allowed to feel without being punished. That's why, after our children have acknowledged their own emotions about a given situation, we coach them on how to step into the shoes of others and consider their emotions.

If we punish, dismiss, or minimize our children's emotions, we run the risk that our kids will ascribe a false narrative to the meaning of their emotions and internalize that narrative, making the situation all about them. This is why we must keep in mind John Gottman's incredible insight, "My child isn't giving me a hard time. My child is having a hard time."[9] Kennedy, in her defiance, was having a hard time. When our kids are anxious, they need someone to help them assign proper meaning to their circumstance, just as God does with us when we verbalize our worries and fears to him in prayer (Philippians 4:6-7).

When you feel overwhelmed by emotion, take it to God first. Then talk to your spouse about what you're feeling. Be available for your kids and encourage them to talk about their feelings as well. When you make it normal and safe to talk about emotions in your home, you get to see deeper into the hearts of those you love. The more you put feeling words to your experiences as a family, the more connected you'll become. And when those you love feel seen and heard, they'll know they're center stage.

12

DECISION 4: LISTEN TO YOUR SPOUSE'S HEART

How 15 Minutes a Day Can Change Your Marriage

CHRISTI

I want to go back to where it all began for us, the moment Josh sauntered into the house accompanied by the smell of his fresh latte, telling me about his exciting projects, as I stood in the kitchen spackled with banana and sweet potato. I felt frazzled, anxious, unkempt, and achingly alone in my early years of motherhood. That's when I lashed out with, "Why do you never ask me about me? It's always about you. You never ask about what's on my heart."

Not long after that memorable day, Josh left for a week to attend a conference called Ultimate Leadership hosted by Drs. John Townsend and Henry Cloud. John Townsend has been a dear friend and mentor of Josh's for many years, and he urged him to attend. Knowing the season of life we were in, John assured me that a stressful week of me solo parenting would pale in comparison to the ten years of growth we'd see from Josh's week away. I'm glad I listened to him.

When Josh came home from Ultimate Leadership, he said, "Christi, I learned a lot about good leadership, but I was burdened by how poorly I was leading in our home. When you challenged me about not inquiring about your heart, I felt ashamed. I had no clue where to begin or what that even looked like. But I think I have an idea that might help. Would you be willing to try something with me?"

First of all, Josh felt ashamed?

I didn't know that. He always seemed so confident. Looking back, I think what came across as confidence was really shame disguised as defensiveness. It wasn't true confidence. I had my own insecurities, so I questioned myself more than I did Josh. The fruit of that dance between us led to a pattern of surface-level conversation and further disconnection.

Josh explained how he'd realized that when he processed his day with me, it was mostly content-based (information about what he did, who he talked to, etc.) rather than process-based (what he *felt* about what he did or who he talked to). Now, here he stood, revealing a deeper layer of his heart to me. Why wouldn't I want to give his idea a try? His vulnerability made me want to fight *for* him. My only hesitation was wondering if his idea was an after-conference high that would fade into oblivion after a week. But what did I have to lose?

So began the foundational practice we call "15 Minutes a Day," which is how we implement Decision 4: Listen to Your Spouse's Heart. Although it felt awkward and clunky at first, it wasn't long before it moved from a formal exercise to a natural lifestyle in our home. We pray it becomes a lifestyle in your home as well.

15 Minutes a Day

Fifteen Minutes a Day is a proactive way to put your spouse center stage, an exercise focusing on what's going on *within* your spouse's heart more than what's going on *between* the two of you. Remember, great communication happens when we fight for each other, not against each other. And we're much more likely to fight for each other when we see what's really going on under the surface.

Practicing 15 Minutes a Day is about as straightforward as it sounds. You simply set aside time each day to talk about the emotions you experienced that day. The exercise is simple. The daily investment is doable. And the reward on the investment is an ongoing deepening connection you won't achieve by living on the surface.

Start by choosing the time of day that works best for both of you. Most couples choose either the end of the day or the beginning of the day. For example, instead of mindlessly numbing out on Netflix or social media after the kids go to bed, set aside fifteen minutes to talk to each other. If the morning works best, set aside fifteen minutes over coffee before the kids wake up. Regardless, be intentional. Some couples lament, "We don't have fifteen minutes in a day." Our response: no excuses. As Josh puts it, "If marital connection were a sport and I were your coach, I wouldn't put you and your spouse in the game unless you practiced this exercise every single day. You can't win without the fundamentals." It's not a matter of having the time; it's a matter of making the time. Being famous at home requires intentionality.

Next, decide who will speak first and who will listen first. Halfway through your fifteen minutes, you'll switch to allow the other spouse to share.

When you are the speaker, share one positive emotion and

one negative or uncomfortable emotion you experienced that day. When you first start using this practice, we recommend choosing something from your day that's unrelated to anything going on in your relationship. For positive emotions, you might share when you felt "excited," "happy," "joyful," "hopeful," etc. For negative or uncomfortable emotions, you might share anything that made you feel "rejected," "sad," "angry," or "jealous." Feel free to use the feelings chart from the previous chapter.

In the beginning, many people we coach find it helpful to use phrases such as, "I felt relieved and happy when" or "I felt embarrassed when." Then they describe the event that made them feel that way. Simply using feeling words engages both sides of the brain, which not only strengthens your bond but deepens your intimacy level together.

If you need a few prompts to get started, you can ask each other questions. For example:

- What's on your heart today?
- What was the highlight of your day? How did you feel about that?
- How did this person/project/meeting make you feel?
- What was the most challenging part of your day? How did you feel?
- How do you feel right now?
- When did your heart come alive today?

Here's the kicker: You are not allowed to engage in fixing or problem-solving during your fifteen minutes. That means you offer no advice, no suggestions, no solutions. You simply sit with your spouse and listen attentively to his or her feelings from the day. Don't fix it; just validate it.

Tips to Make It Work for You

You have to practice, practice, practice each day. If you don't make 15 Minutes a Day a lifestyle in your relationship, it'll fade out faster than tight-rolled jeans. Here are a few tips to keep in mind.

Talk about how you feel about feelings. Although the basic practice is to share a positive and a negative emotion for the day, you could use one of your first 15 Minutes a Day sessions to talk about how you feel about feelings. For example, on a scale of one to ten, how comfortable are you using feeling words when talking about something that's important to you? Were you allowed to use feeling words growing up? Why or why not? Talk about any reservations you might have. This is what 15 Minutes a Day is all about—cultivating a safe space for both of you to feel comfortable talking about emotions.

Don't make it any more awkward than it needs to be. You don't have to stare into the eyes of your beloved to do this exercise. Now that it's become a lifestyle, we often have our conversations while unloading the dishwasher, making dinner, or even over video calls if Josh is out of town.

Don't be legalistic about the time. Just because we call it 15 Minutes a Day doesn't mean it always has to literally be fifteen minutes. Sometimes Josh and I share our hearts with each other in just a few minutes, and other times it takes much longer. When the pandemic hit in March 2020 and we were in the middle of lockdowns, one of our fifteen minutes turned into a two-hour tear fest. Okay, I did most of the crying, but I needed to process all of the changes the lockdown threw into our laps. Though we had never previously set aside two hours for heart-to-heart conversation, apart from a date night, we needed more time during that stressful season. And some of those longer conversations became turning points at crucial moments in the life of our family. Had we not set aside time for 15 Minutes a Day, we might have missed out on conversations we wouldn't otherwise know we needed to have.

Share your feelings about each other. Once you've been practicing 15 Minutes a Day for a while and you feel brave and ready, share the feelings you experienced toward your spouse that day. Did your spouse say or do something that encouraged or validated you? Tell your spouse how it made you feel. So often, our spouse will make our heart come alive by something they said or did, but we neglect to acknowledge it, either out of busyness or distraction.

Or did your spouse say or do anything that discouraged or invalidated you? Again, tell your spouse how it made you feel. When you are the listener, remember to focus on your spouse's feelings without getting defensive and without trying to fix the situation. The admonition of Scripture is, "Be quick to listen, slow to speak, and slow to get angry. Human anger does not produce the righteousness God desires" (James 1:19-20).

When you are the person sharing your feelings, remember that you have to be willing to give up blame and refrain from making accusations. For example, saying, "I feel angry because you never want to spend time with me," is sure to put the walls up around your spouse's heart. Using "you" is an accusation. Instead, use "I" statements to convey the negative feeling and pair it with a pro-relationship thought or positive desire about the relationship. For example, "I feel alone and really miss being with you. I would love to discover hobbies we can do together."

Make adjustments. As you continue to practice 15 Minutes a Day, feel free to make adjustments. Josh and I no longer have a set time, but it's become natural for us to check in on the other's heart throughout the day. Sometimes that's via text, on the phone while driving to activities, during meal prep, or as we're going to bed.

We're at a point now where we know if we need a sit-down to go deeper. As you practice 15 Minutes a Day, you'll find your rhythm. Some of these questions might help you get started.

- What was it like to do 15 Minutes a Day the first time? Was it easier or more difficult than you imagined it would be? Why?
- What, if anything, surprised you about 15 Minutes a Day?
- What did you learn about your spouse? What did you learn about yourself?
- What is one thing you can do to make sure this practice becomes a daily habit?

Use these tips to help you make 15 Minutes a Day a lifestyle that works for you. As a bonus, you'll likely find yourself becoming more aware of your own emotions and how people and events influence how you feel and show up at home each day. With daily practice, it can pull you out of a state of emotional dullness by strengthening your ability to recognize your own emotions. When someone asks how you feel, most of the time you might say, "I'm good. Busy. Fine." But none of those are feeling words. It takes vulnerability to say something like, "I felt disappointed today because of a friend who dismissed me."

The more you get to know what's happening within the deeper recesses of your spouse's heart, the more aware you become of who your spouse is. Being vulnerable and giving voice to how much you value the relationship helps you to better fight for each other, not against each other. As followers of Jesus, we want our marriage to reflect God's unwavering love for us, to be a relationship so alive and abundant that people ask us the reason for the love we have for each other.

Bringing Calm in Reactive Moments

JOSH

To be clear, a fifteen-minute daily conversation isn't going to eliminate all your arguments as a couple. However, we have found that it can decrease the number of blowups couples have over time and help couples resolve those blowups much more quickly. So how do we use the Seven Decisions to bring calm and be emotionally safe during reactive moments? Here's one example.

A few years ago, I was in the middle of a very busy travel season, and I was missing Christi. Like, really missing her. I was flying home on a Wednesday, and I planned to take her out for a dinner date on Thursday so we could reconnect. However, because of my schedule that week, we had let our 15 Minutes a Day slip a little bit. I hadn't communicated as well as I could have about feeling disconnected or about my plan to take her out on a date the night after I got home.

I had also forgotten that, on the day I arrived home, we had already planned for two of our closest couple friends and their kids to come over for dinner. After dinner, we gathered in the living room for coffee while the kids played upstairs. Remember, the story I'm telling myself at this point is that I am taking Christi on a date night tomorrow night. However, as the three women were sitting around the cozy fireplace with coffees in hand, I overheard them talking about their planned girls' night out—for Thursday night!

What did I hear? I heard that Christi hadn't missed me the way I had missed her. She hadn't even bothered to tell me about her plans.

Have you ever had the experience of remembering what you said, but forgetting how you said it? Or has your version of how you said something been the polar opposite of your spouse's version? Yeah. This was the point where our stories diverged.

Feeling hurt and disconnected, I confronted Christi in front of everyone, "Why didn't you tell me you were going out with your friends tomorrow night?" I don't remember the tone or volume of my voice, or my facial expression, body language, eye contact, or any of the other nonverbal signals I sent. But Christi did. She *felt* all of it.

Now, not only did I feel disconnected, I also felt wronged. And though I didn't know what was happening at the time, or even why, I felt Christi shut down.

Maybe you've been there. You feel the tension as you fake your smile and usher your friends out the door, "Good night! That was fun!"

As soon as the door closed, it felt like *Frozen 2*, with ice forming down the walls of our home. Not a word was spoken.

As Christi went upstairs to get ready for bed, I locked the doors, turned out the lights, and planned in my head just exactly how I was going to approach her with my lonely, disconnected-turned-angry feelings toward her. I had made an accusation I now needed to address. Making my way upstairs, I was armed with words. But as I turned to walk into the bathroom, Christi turned her head toward me and said, "Don't you *ever* speak to me that way in front of our friends again."

I still remember her tone of voice.

Speechless, I walked past her into our closet. Seething. I had an accusation against her, and now she was throwing one at me?

Welcome to a reactive moment—the moment when your survival response is triggered. You feel wronged. Ready to self-protect. Primed to jump into your dysfunctional dance. In that moment, you can react by fighting, fleeing, or freezing. Or you can stop and do three things: 1) choose to endure the negative emotion, 2) change the only person you can, and 3) give up accusation and blame. Now you see why we're so big on you entering your own story, paying attention to your own emotions, and practicing 15 Minutes a Day—so you already have an idea of what's going on within your spouse's heart in these moments.

Standing in my closet, I had a decision to make. I could go back into the bathroom and present my offense, or I could go back into the bathroom and listen to Christi's criticism. Remember, the instinctual, primitive part of the brain was triggered in both of us at that moment, which meant we were both in survival mode and operating by instinct, not higher thought.[1]

One of the tools we use to help couples process reactive moments after the fact is a Relationship Moment Worksheet, which you can download at famousathome.com/book. The worksheet has three columns: "What Your Spouse Said," "What You Said," and "Your Spouse's Response."[2] In each column, couples write down precisely what was said, and only what was said. No commentary or interpretation. Just the word-for-word accusation or criticism.

What Your Spouse Said	What You Said	Your Spouse's Response

The worksheet is designed to help you see exactly what was said in the moment and to identify a response (the middle column) that enables you to fight for your spouse's heart, not against your spouse's heart by blaming or overreacting. I'm going to walk through the worksheet to explore two different options for how I might have responded to Christi's accusation: "Don't you *ever* speak to me that way again."

I knew I could not change Christi. Though I disagreed with her assessment of how harsh I'd come across in front of our friends, there was no disagreeing with how she felt—embarrassed and belittled. I had to put aside my story to enter hers—an incredibly difficult endeavor when I already felt accused.

Using the worksheet, I've written Christi's accusation in the first column. She accused me of speaking harshly to her in front of our friends: "Don't you *ever* speak to me that way again." I have two choices for how I can respond to Christi. Though I can't change her, I do have the power to influence the response I might get from her in column three by what I say in column two.

Everything in me wanted to *react* from my own story—from fight, flight, or freeze mode—to tell her how much I obviously missed her more than she was missing me (sarcasm). Let's say for the sake of the example that I came out of my closet and reacted with my own accusation: "You could have avoided this if you had told me your schedule."

What Your Spouse Said	What You Said	Your Spouse's Response
"Don't you **ever** speak to me that way again."	"You could have avoided this if you had told me your schedule."	

What one word do you see repeated in column two?

You.

What does "you" represent? Blame.

What direction do you suppose this conversation is heading if I choose to react from my own story? Not in a healthy one. Most likely another accusation from Christi, which might have looked like this.

What Your Spouse Said	What You Said	Your Spouse's Response
"Don't you **ever** speak to me that way again."	"You could have avoided this if you had told me your schedule."	"Can't you even see how awkward that was? How it made me feel?"

Keep in mind, I had come home with a story I was already telling myself. I also felt wronged, and I wanted to make it known. But unless I pursued her story and focused on listening to her heart, my story wouldn't be heard.

Back to me in the closet. While I was standing there staring at my clothes, I was mentally walking through my willingness to endure the uncomfortable emotions of this conversation, to give up blame, and to change myself.

Let's look at the chart again. This time, I'll use "I" feeling statements, pro-relationship thoughts, and empathy to respond to Christi's story in column two.[3] I may not remember coming across as harshly as Christi accused me of being, but I have to enter her story and acknowledge my role in her pain because she's feeling it. If I ignore her pain, I'll only ramp up the response in column three. This is why empathy is so important.

What Your Spouse Said	What You Said	Your Spouse's Response
"Don't you **ever** speak to me that way again."	"I'm sorry I hurt you like that. I was really looking forward to a date night tomorrow night because I missed you. I'm sorry my disappointment came out in such a hurtful way in front of our friends."	

What one word repeats in column two this time?

I.

What does "I" represent? Taking responsibility for feelings and actions.

What direction do you suppose this conversation is heading? A much better one, which might have looked like this.

What Your Spouse Said	What You Said	Your Spouse's Response
"Don't you **ever** speak to me that way again."	"I'm sorry I hurt you like that. I was really looking forward to a date night tomorrow night because I missed you. I'm sorry my disappointment came out in such a hurtful way in front of our friends."	"I didn't realize you were thinking of a date night or that you missed me as much as you did."

Though the hurt feelings will take some work to resolve, it will be much quicker than blaming and fighting for myself instead of fighting for Christi's heart and our relationship.

I had to go into my closet to calm my brain that night so I'd respond in a helpful way, not a hurtful one—thinking about and pursuing 100 percent what was going on within Christi's heart. But it required me standing in my closet, closing my eyes, and imagining the word *you* in that second column like a blinking neon sign. Having just come off the road speaking about how to do this very exercise, I knew I needed to practice what I preached. I went out and fought for Christi's heart that night, even though I felt wronged. I had to see the grain of truth in Christi's accusation. I knew we'd resolve our differing stories much sooner if I were willing to enter hers. That was one night I actually got it right.

When you do this worksheet together, usually long enough after an argument that you've both calmed down, I recommend putting yourself in the second column so you can reflect on how you responded or reacted in the moment to your spouse's criticism. When we're in a heated moment, accusations fly both ways. Go back to the exact moment, put one of your spouse's criticisms in the first column, then write out how you reacted.

Whenever the reactive moments hit, think, *How can I respond rather than react?* Or, if it helps, think of the "You" in the middle column as a blinking neon sign. If you find yourselves going into your normal dysfunctional dance, because you will, sit down once you're both calm and map out the moment—what was said word for word, and how you can better focus on what's going on *within* your spouse's heart next time.

You can probably see how proactively practicing 15 Minutes a Day—when your brain is calm and your defenses are down—helps you respond to your spouse's story in reactive moments when your brain is ramped up. Doing the Relationship Moment Worksheet after an argument can help you interrupt your normal relational dance. Too often after an argument, couples just go their separate ways and rarely come back to how they spoke to each other and the deeper feelings they had about the situation. Instead, these exercises help you connect the right and left sides of the brain so you start to think more deeply about what happened and how you can show up focused on your spouse's heart the next time. Doing this helps you write a more coherent and life-giving marital story.

By now, I hope you're beginning to see how all of this is coming together—how taking responsibility for your actions and entering your spouse's story enable you to listen to your spouse's heart. That's how you put your marriage center stage.

13

DECISION 5: ENTER YOUR CHILD'S WORLD

How 20 Minutes a Day Can Fuel Your Child's Soul

JOSH

A mom of three approached me after a parenting event, distraught about a behavior regression happening with her middle son. Over the previous few weeks, he had uncharacteristically begun protesting her departure when she dropped him off at kindergarten. By the time she shared her concerns with me, he was kicking and flailing his arms and had injured his teacher. Mom was worried.

I began with my normal line of questioning: When did this start? What, if any, significant life events or changes happened around that time? What patterns, if any, were interrupted?

As it turned out, her oldest child had been in the hospital for surgery. Her youngest was a breastfeeding newborn. With Mom having spent so much time at the hospital the past few weeks, guess who was getting the least of her affection—and her normal attention? The one kicking and screaming at her departure.

"How much time have you been getting with your middle child?" I asked.

"Not much at all, actually," she answered. "I feel horrible, but it's been so hard with my oldest in the hospital."

"I can't imagine. I bet you miss him too," I said.

Tears filled her eyes. "I do. And I feel like I'm failing all of them."

"May I make a suggestion?" I asked.

"Yes, please."

"Do you have twenty minutes of your day you could carve out to just be with your middle son? Like a mom-son date each day for twenty minutes? No distractions. You enter his world and play with him, doing what he wants to do. If it's building a tower, build a tower. If it's racing cars on a track, pick the most colorful car. If it's playing a game, play it on the floor.[1] But let him lead the play."

She thought about it for a minute. "Well, he is the first one up in the morning. I could wake up earlier to get ready for the day and spend one-on-one time with him instead of using that time to get ready."

For the next week, she carved out an additional twenty minutes in her morning to spend one-on-one time with her boy before school. When I checked in a week later, her son's behaviors at drop-off were back to normal.

I share this story not because I believe twenty minutes a day is a magic pill for all your parenting problems. But it is what your children desire: uninterrupted, undistracted time with their greatest hero—you. This is why raising great kids is a process of becoming—first becoming a more self-aware individual and then becoming an emotionally safe and grounding presence for your kids.

Decision 5: Enter Your Child's World is the great equalizer, the one decision you can use to create a lifestyle of simple but life-changing moments with your kids. And 20 Minutes a Day is one of the best practices we know for putting in the time to be an overnight success a decade in the making.

If fame in the world comes by inspiring others, then fame at home comes by inspiring your child. As child development researcher Stanley Greenspan writes, "Bright, emotionally healthy, and moral children don't just happen. . . . All the wonderful things you wish for your child do not have to be left to chance, intuition, or genetic endowment. Nor do they require hours of flash cards, educational TV, or special computer-based learning exercises."[2] What it requires is for you, the parent, to be face-to-face with your children, entering their worlds with no distractions. Your children don't need another program; they simply need your presence.

When you are committed to doing the work of becoming, you learn how showing up undistracted to champion what each of your children loves helps calm their emotionally overwhelmed brains and lead to the outcomes you desire most in your children.

Four Ways to Enter Your Child's World

Every day, Christi and I ask ourselves if we made these decisions: *Did I get fifteen minutes with my spouse? Did I get twenty minutes with each of my children?* The goal is to hold to the principle but not beat ourselves up if we can't get twenty minutes with every child every day. In fact, if you have eight, nine, or twelve kids, Lord bless you. It's impossible. But ask yourself, "Who needs my time the most today? Tomorrow? Which child is feeling off? Whom do I feel the most distance with right now?" Start with that child.

Just as there will be days when you spend less than fifteen minutes talking about emotions with your spouse, there will also be days when twenty minutes with your child could be ten minutes, like the Uno game I had on the stairs with Kennedy before my livestream speaking event. Or your time could turn into an hour or more. The aim, though, is a doable and consistent twenty minutes a day.

Our kids need us to enter their world, and we do that best when we aim for twenty minutes a day with our children, doing what they love. Greenspan calls this "command-free time."[3] You make no commands; you just enter your child's world. You become a student of your child. If you practice 20 Minutes a Day, over time you'll get really good at being able to champion your child's interests and strengths, calm their brain, coach their challenges, and right your wrongs—four ways you can enter your child's world.

1. Champion Their Interests and Strengths

A few years ago, my friend Frank flew into town to stay with us while working on a book project I was helping him with. Having flown in on a red-eye from California to Nashville, he arrived at our house early one morning feeling groggy and ready for coffee. By 7:30 a.m., Landon, who was four at the time, was awake and dancing around the house with a guitar, singing as loudly as his little vocal cords allowed. Frank was all the audience Landon needed to perform his new song. I apologized to Frank and told Landon to stop.

As I got Frank his coffee, I heard Landon finish his song and say, "Do you want to hear another one?"

I interrupted. "No, buddy. Mr. Frank needs his coffee. Let's turn it off now."

As I turned around, I saw Frank look Landon in the eyes. "I would *love* to hear another song. Can I get a cup of coffee first?"

Walking over, I apologized again. "No, Landon. Mr. Frank is good. Let's go find something else to do."

This time, Frank interrupted me. "No, Landon, let's hear your next song. I'm ready now."

I thought Frank was just being nice and argued with him not to oblige.

"Josh," he said, "you have no idea. Being in the music industry, I don't often see four-year-olds with this kind of enthusiasm for an audience and singing their own lyrics. You need to champion him in what he loves."

"I get it," I said, "but it's 7:30 in the morning and you're our guest."

I guess I didn't fully get it. "Josh, what annoys you as a parent is usually the very activity your child is passionate about or good at," Frank said. "You get annoyed because you don't understand."

I had to sit on this entire exchange for a while. The way Frank entered Landon's world. How he wasn't annoyed by the behavior but championed it. How he enlivened Landon's heart while I tried to shut it down.

At the time, Landon was also playing T-ball. A few months later when it came time to sign him up for the fall season, I remembered that moment between Landon and Frank. This was the moment I realized Landon really wasn't into T-ball the way I wanted him to be.

"Buddy, it's time to sign up for T-ball again. Would you rather play T-ball or take guitar lessons?"

He got a grin as wide as the Mississippi. "I want to take guitar lessons, Dad!"

Thus began my journey to celebrating my kids for who they are, not mourning who they're not.[4] It's possible for us to get so stuck in our own story that we cripple our child's story, especially when we're more focused on mourning who they're not rather than celebrating who God made them to be.

A concerned mom once approached me after a speaking engagement. "Josh, can you help me?" she asked. "My son is learning to rap, and I don't know what to do. I don't like that kind of music."

I went through a line of questioning to see if there was a deeper concern.

"Is he hanging out with kids he shouldn't be? The Bible says, 'Bad company corrupts good character.'"

"No," she replied. "He has good friends. They're all in the same youth group."

"Is he listening to music that degrades women or promotes violence?" I asked.

"No," she said a bit sheepishly. "He listens to Christian rap."

"Then I only have one piece of advice for you," I said boldly. "Learn how to rap."

If we don't pursue our kids' interests and champion who God created *them* to be, they'll find somebody who will, which only builds a massive wall between their heart and ours.

One other way to bring your child's heart alive is to use what my friend Frank described in that book he wrote as "data-based praise," or the "I was bragging about you today" technique. Solomon wrote, "Wisdom shouts in the streets. She cries out in the public square" (Proverbs 1:20). I believe if we pay attention, our kids scream data at us all the time about their interests, strengths, and gifts. Such wisdom about who our children are becoming is gold. But, as Frank lamented, we cannot hear their "screaming data" if we, the adults, are the ones "screaming data."[5] Find something your child is either good at or works really hard at, then tell them that you bragged about them to someone else. Be specific. This isn't about giving false praise or making broad-stroke affirmations such as, "Son, you are really smart." Instead, be specific about the effort, insight, or talent. Praise the data.

Distracted and busy, we so often miss these moments, passing along what can feel like an insincere, "Good job, honey," as we continue onto our next task or email or scroll through social media. If you have trouble finding twenty minutes, check your screen time app and steal twenty minutes away from it. Remember, the Seven Decisions are about no longer conforming to the patterns of this world but being transformed by the renewing of your mind (Romans 12:2). That's what it means to be famous at home.

2. Calm Their Brain

When kids feel emotionally secure, they explore the world around them. But when exploration leads to a threat that triggers their fight, flight, or freeze response, whom do they look to for help to calm their overwhelmed brain? You.

Did you ever get lost in a grocery store or amusement park as a child? You turned around and Mom and Dad were missing. What happened within your body? Your heart rate sped up. You got butterflies in your stomach. And what was the first action you took? You tried to find Mom and Dad. Your parents' presence in those overwhelming moments had a calming effect on your brain. Once you felt safe again, you went back to exploring the world around you.[6]

Since exploration leads to self-confidence and self-competence later in life,[7] seeking to understand what's happening in the inner world of our child's emotions sets the stage for their long-term ability to manage stress and successfully problem-solve under pressure. In a finite way, by helping our child organize their feelings, we provide peace to calm their anxious brain. In our work with families, Christi and I find the best way to calm a child's emotional overwhelm is to lead in grace and follow in truth—an approach that may not always feel like the best one in the moment. At least that's how it felt to my friend Kyle when he had a difficult encounter with one of his kids.

Kyle called me angry and confused about what to do with his fourteen-year-old daughter, Sarah, who had asked to go to a Friday night football game. When he told her no, she screamed, "Dad, I hate you!" and went storming to her room. He was shocked, the bottom part of *his* brain now triggered. See why parenting is the art of becoming? Reacting from his own fear would only have served to further shut down his daughter. This is why Decision 3: Talk about Emotions precedes Decision 5: Enter Your Child's World. We have to be comfortable entering the emotional worlds of our kids.

At this point, Kyle had to decide how to respond.

He could *ignore* Sarah's emotions by dropping the issue to avoid further conflict.

He could *dismiss* her emotions by saying, "Don't be mad at me."

He could *minimize* her emotions by saying, "It's just a football game. Who cares?"

He could *punish* her emotions by shutting her down and yelling, "Don't you ever speak to me that way again. I'm taking your phone for a month. And *no*! You're not going to that football game! *Do you understand me*?!"

But to lead in grace and calm Sarah's emotional overwhelm is to enter her world as a safe sounding board and to help her organize what's happening in the right side of her brain. As parents, we have the privilege of helping our kids write beautiful stories by putting language to what's happening within their hearts.

A safe way for Kyle to show up in a moment like this is to get on his daughter's eye level, enter her world, and ask, "Honey, what is it about that Friday night football game that matters so much to you?"

When Kyle did that, he found out Sarah had been rejected by a group of friends. She'd seen them on social media posting pictures of hanging out together without her. This was the first Friday night she'd been invited to be a part of the group, and her dad had said no.

Anger precedes the real pain. There's another emotion behind the anger. But so often as parents, instead of entering our child's story, we lead with hard truth, punishing our child's angry response because, "In no way will my child ever speak to me like that." Leading in truth, we react in both fear and pride.

But as my friend John Townsend says, truth without grace leads to condemnation.[9] And when our children feel condemned, it only builds a higher wall between their hearts and ours. Leading in grace requires stepping into our child's story and seeking to understand before being understood. Not until we feel understood do our hearts open to understanding. Sometimes our best twenty minutes with our kids happens when we tend to their fearful or angry heart at the end of the day, taking extra time to enter their world as we tuck them into bed at night. [8]

3. Coach Their Challenges

But what about following with truth, you might ask? What about discipline? As your children grow, the twenty minutes a day you spend entering their world will create an atmosphere of trust, keeping your children open-minded as you coach them through life's challenges. And you'll want to have that atmosphere of trust for the times you need to follow with truth and discipline.

I don't think we struggle with disciplining kids as much as we think we do in the moment. Though exceptions exist because every child has a free will, most discipline issues stem either from an overabundance of grace to the neglect of truth, or from grace drowned under the weight of truth. The real struggle for many of us as parents isn't saying no to our kids; it's being okay with saying yes and taking the time to enter their world. That's what Decision 5 is all about.

Kyle allowed Sarah to go to the football game but not until they talked about it and searched for a solution. He listened to what she wanted to do and why. He then shared his concerns that Sarah's friends might reject her at the game. They worked together and came up with a plan. After the game, Sarah had consequences because of the disrespectful way she had reacted to her dad.

I'm of the Fred Rogers persuasion on the topic of discipline. He said, "I think of discipline as the continual everyday process of helping a child learn self-discipline." If my kids become who I am, my own self-discipline lived in front of my kids matters more in the long run than a consequence in the moment. I can't discipline my kids about money if I'm a wasteful spender, discipline them about kindness if I'm acting like a jerk to their mom, or discipline them about a healthy lifestyle if I'm not exercising while simultaneously stuffing my face full of chips (my self-confessed weakness).

Sometimes, you'll need more than twenty-minutes to enter your child's world so you can both calm their brain and explain the consequence (with younger children), or problem-solve for a solution and proper consequence (with teens). For example, when your kids bicker and fight, think of coaching through the challenge rather than disciplining the bickering. Use the Golden Rule. Ask your children how they can make it right. What Bible verse might apply? You can also use this time to role-play with your children. What happens if you get bullied at school or on the playground by another kid? Do you tell Mom and Dad? Role-playing at home gives your children the tools for handling difficult emotions and situations as they grow older and don't have you nearby. All it takes is a lifestyle of twenty minutes a day of entering their world.

Christi and I follow three coaching principles for our own discipline. *Be clear. Be consistent. And follow through.* When we do struggle with discipline it's typically because we weren't clear on the rules with our kids, weren't consistent in implementing the rules, or failed to follow through with a consequence. If we send mixed messages to our kids about the rules, how will they know what they can and cannot do? And we have to be consistent in applying the same three rules to our own life discipline. Are we clear and consistent, and do we follow through on our own rules and convictions?

Kids follow our lead more than our words.

4. Right Your Wrongs

Entering your child's world also requires the humility to right your wrongs.

When Landon and Kennedy were in their preschool years, we had a daily parenting routine. Christi had the kids during the day, and I'd take over when I was home and done with work to handle bath and bed at night. On the days both kids attended their four-hour preschool, they missed their naps. At the preschool age, overtired means extra energy and extra decibels. It was bedtime on one of those preschool days, and Christi was ready for quiet. Calling my attention to the fact that it was time to tuck the kids into bed, she waltzed into the laundry room to take a deep breath while folding the laundry (one of the tasks no one loves but at least you can do alone).

To add context to the story, I get overstimulated by loud noises. I love the quiet so much I often drive with no music or radio. Just me and the stillness. I know. Not a great temperament type for dealing with loud and overtired preschoolers.

Since Landon's bedroom is across the hall from the laundry room, Christi was privy to the decibel levels of two overtired kids who were now my sole responsibility. I initially felt like I had everything under control. I like bedtime. I live for the tickles, cuddles, and prayers. But I wasn't moving fast enough for an already overwhelmed Christi. As I stood in the hallway, she stepped out of the laundry room holding a half-folded towel. "Can you do something with them?" she quipped, a decibel level higher than the kids' squeals so she could get my attention.

Since she was speaking at that level, guess where the kids' decibel level went next? Higher than hers.

Guess who gets overstimulated by loud noise? This guy.

At that moment, I had to go a decibel even higher to calm my overstimulated brain. Yes, my fight, flight, freeze response overreacted. I yelled.

"STOP! EVERYBODY STOP!"

I'm not a yeller, so you can imagine what happened next in my children's worlds. When I looked down, I saw Landon's bottom lip begin to quiver and tears start to spill down his cheeks. Kennedy held a thousand-yard stare, her little mind trying to process what had just happened. Two kids were just being kids and getting yelled at for it.

In that moment, I had to get down on my knees, look my children in the eyes, and enter their worlds.

Let's get real. You will yell, say things you regret, and overreact to your kids. You're human. Your fight, flight, or freeze response isn't always going to be calm in the moment. But stay with me. What you're about to read may free you.

When the bedtime decibel levels were off the charts and I yelled at everyone in the house, I became the threat, the source of my kids' triggered fear response. What happens when the source of our kids' safety and calm also becomes the threat? We must right our wrongs. When this happens, the two most powerful words a parent can say to a child are, "I'm sorry."

Research shows that if we can show up in an emotionally safe way for our kids even 40 percent of the time, we can still get the outcomes we desire. Come on, friend! That should encourage you. Even Shaq shot better than 40 percent from the free throw line. Why just four out of ten times? Because research shows a word called "repair" is the "ultimate" of relationships.[10] Guess what the Bible calls it? Forgiveness. And Jesus told us to practice it a lot!

Saying "I'm sorry" to Landon and Kennedy about my specific offense and asking how I could make it right in that moment sent three powerful messages:

1. I'm not perfect.
2. I don't expect you to be perfect.
3. This is how you make things right when they're not.

Making it right with the kids was one thing. Entering Christi's world afterward was another. Excuse me as I go crawl into the dryer and close the door behind me.

You are the apple of your child's eye, the most famous person in the world to them. So as you consider practicing 20 Minutes a Day to enter your child's world, focus on what your kids get excited about. What brings them to life? What are they good at? What data are they showing you about who they are and what they love? Are you giving your kids opportunities to do those activities? How can you join them?

Watch what happens to your kids when you make the decision to enter their world for twenty minutes a day. Look for changes in their attitude, mood, or behavior. Again, I'm not saying 20

Minutes a Day will solve all of your behavioral issues, but just think about how you feel when other people champion what you love, the encouragement you receive when someone acknowledges your strengths, and how you calm down when others comfort you in your overwhelm. Imagine how much more it fuels your child's soul when it's their greatest hero who enters their world to champion, calm, and coach them.

14

DECISION 6: ESTABLISH FAMILY RHYTHMS

How to Embrace the Moment While Living for the Decade

CHRISTI

A few years ago, I came across a Pinterest board by a woman who created meticulous schedules, all of which were collected in various binders. The cleaning binder especially caught my attention, as it contained a daily plan for keeping her house spotless. Even I, a type A personality who loves lists, felt suffocated by the picture.

To help me reconcile my disorganized chaos with the tidy harmony of the moms I couldn't keep up with, I made fun of the binders and schedules. "I need room to breathe," I reasoned. Besides, I was organized. I kept lists. But I didn't have any overriding goal or purpose for where my lists were taking me. I made fun of the "scheduler mom," but I couldn't see then how, in the name of "spontaneity," my inability to tell my time where to go left me even more exhausted, always playing catch-up, and aching for even a minute's rest.

I was tired of feeling victimized by my schedule. Instead of falling into bed each night and celebrating the few sweet moments of connection I had enjoyed, I ended most days lamenting and longing for more meaningful moments with Josh and the kids. I was starting to worry that if things didn't change, I'd wake up one day to an empty nest having "missed it."

Missed *what* exactly, I wasn't sure. I just felt an ache I knew was anything but a spirit of peace. And it wasn't happiness I was chasing. In place of the ache, I wanted to feel something much deeper.

Fulfilled.

Peaceful.

Content.

Grounded.

I liked those words a lot. Those were the deeper feelings I wanted to have when I put my head on the pillow each night.

And every now and then, I did feel that way. I just didn't know why. What was different about the days I went to bed feeling fulfilled versus the days I went to bed feeling inadequate? What I ultimately discovered was that the days I felt fulfilled were the days I left room to either create a meaningful moment or to show up in an unplanned moment.

Moments Matter

Moments matter. Sadly, we live such busy lives we miss many of them. Families who don't take time to rest and celebrate get caught up in the cultural tide of making "so busy" the badge-of-honor answer to the question, "How are you?"

Being busy is not a badge of honor. It's the foe of memorable moments. Busyness kills celebration. And yet, some of the most productive and fulfilled people I know prioritize celebration.

How often do you experience a moment worth celebrating but

move on to the next thing without thinking twice? Did you stop to celebrate when your child learned to tie his shoes or cheerfully shared a toy? Did you pause to take in the moment when you helped a friend through a difficult time, completed a project, or carried out a mission? What about when you wrote a book, released a song, restored your marriage, won an award, paid off a debt, or completed a degree? All of it matters, but rarely is all of it celebrated.

We minimize our value in the world when we quickly jump from one item to the next on the to-do list. Sure, we might get a lot a done. I did. But rarely did I feel truly fulfilled when my highest goal was simply to complete the task and check it off my list. With whom did I share the moment? Whom was it for? Why did I complete it? Did it even matter?

However important the task may have been, it didn't matter if doing it undermined my relationships—including the relationship I have with myself.

I started to imagine something different for my life. I wanted time for moments. Time to celebrate the good I put into the world. Time to acknowledge the daily wins I saw in Josh. Time to praise a new milestone or growth opportunity in our kids. But that could only happen if I created margin for the moments. I knew we had to take authority over our schedules so we could live as human beings, not human doings.

Though I'll never have a cleaning binder, my life today looks a lot less like disorganized chaos and a lot more like that Pinterest scheduler than I ever imagined it would. And no one is more surprised than spontaneous me that what made it all possible is Decision 6: Establish Family Rhythms—a combination of daily and weekly rhythms that breathe life into my soul.

Family rhythms provide the oxygen we need to breathe so we can luxuriate in the moments that make us famous at home.

The Origin of Rhythms

God created the natural world with a cosmic rhythm of sunsets and sunrises that mark time into days, weeks, months, and years. He also embedded rhythms into human bodies. Consider the cadence of your heartbeat. The whooshing pulse of blood flowing through your veins. The tempo of breathing in and breathing out. Unbroken physical rhythms are what keep your body fully alive.

God also created rhythms to keep us emotionally and spiritually alive in a chaotic, 24-7 world. With the rising and setting of the sun, the God of the universe created us to live within the boundaries of a seven-day rhythm. He set aside one of those seven days as a Sabbath, a day of rest. And this was part of his plan for us from the very beginning of creation.

In Genesis 1, God created the world as we know it in six days:

Day 1: day and night
Day 2: water and sky
Day 3: plants and trees
Day 4: sun and stars
Day 5: fish and birds
Day 6: animals and humans

Notice what God created first—day and night. The first thing God did was to establish daily rhythms. And then on day four, he created seasonal rhythms with the sun and stars.

When creating day and night, God created light (order) out of darkness (chaos).[1] Darkness comes first. Light, second. This is why Jewish observance of the Sabbath and various holidays begins not at sunrise but at sunset. The traditional Hebrew day begins at sunset because of the creation account, "And there was evening, and there was morning—the first day" (Genesis 1:5, NIV).

Consider for a moment how your life might change if your day started in the evening rather than the morning. Imagine beginning your day at sunset, with the most remarkable meal of the day. After a nourishing dinner with those you love, you then go to bed for an eight-hour sleep. As you wake up, you finish your day by stepping out into the world, onto your stage, doing whatever it is God has called you to.

Sounds lovely, right? That's because God created the day so you could live *from* rest, not *for* it. When you begin the day in the morning, especially with the kids up early, the alarm going off late, or an early commute into the first meeting for the day, you work first, living for the long-fought-after peace and quiet at the end of the day. But when you change your mindset to begin the day in the evening, in rest, the rhythms you create can fuel your soul for the work God has for you each day. Your soul then lives from abundance, not scarcity.

In addition to daily and seasonal rhythms, God's pattern in creation also modeled a pattern of celebration. After each day of creation, God looked back on what he had created and "saw that it was good" (Genesis 1:4, 10, 12, 18, 21, 25, 31). That's celebration.

Then, on the seventh day, God modeled a weekly rhythm by resting from all the work he had done on the previous six days (Genesis 2:3). If God is all-powerful, did he really need to rest? Was he somehow exhausted from his work? Of course not. God rested and celebrated to set a holy rhythm for our lives. And he deemed it all "very good" (Genesis 1:31). During Jesus' earthly ministry, when observance of the Sabbath had deteriorated into an exhausting list of legalisms, he reasserted the purpose of this day of rest: "The Sabbath was made to meet the needs of people, and not people to meet the requirements of the Sabbath" (Mark 2:27).

When we enter into the rhythms God created, we live from rest.

When we resist these rhythms, we live from exhaustion. And when we work but fail to celebrate, we become more like machines than human beings. Machines never stop. Machines never celebrate. Over time, a lack of life rhythms has the power to undermine every aspect of our personhood, beginning with relationships.

That's why family rhythms are so important—they create room for rest. And rest creates margin for moments to breathe and to celebrate the good God is up to in your family, leaving you fulfilled, peaceful, content, and grounded.

Seems like a good way to begin your day as you fall asleep.

Set Your Weekly Rhythm

However chaotic your life might feel right now, you have the authority to create a rhythm for your family. Just as you set a family budget to tell your money where to go, you can set family rhythms to tell your time where to go. If you fail to take authority over your time, you run the risk of living life at the whim of whatever circumstances the day or the week throws your way. In that kind of life, there's no margin for moments. However, when you live by intentional rhythms, you get to live the life you create for yourself.

Josh and I fumbled our way through setting daily rhythms for many years. Then Josh joined a mastermind mentoring group with his friends Jeff Bethke and Jeremy Pryor. When he came home from his first weekend with the group, he was adamant that we put a plan in place to reorder our daily rhythms by starting with weekly ones. Though we'd done okay with our daily rhythms, we weren't ordering our days by beginning with a day of weekly Sabbath rest. The hamster wheel of work and productivity was still the highest priority, and so we allowed the to-do list to determine how much time we had for rest—and it was never enough.

As you begin to set your rhythms, resist the temptation to worry that setting aside a day for rest means essential things will not get done. God can do more with your life in six days than you can do in seven, just as he can do more with 90 percent of your money than you can do with 100 percent of it. Everything you own is his anyway.

Instead of disregarding the divine rhythm God embedded in creation, trust that honoring that rhythm will bring order to your life. The rhythms are meant to serve your family; your family is not made to serve the rhythms. And you can choose the rhythms that work best for you. Rhythms also need to change in different seasons of the year and in different seasons of life. The main thing is to choose a rhythm that works for you and helps you and your spouse to show up in more meaningful ways with each other and with your kids.

So, how exactly do you set up a weekly rhythm? We'll walk through a five-part framework you can use as a starting point. Once you've practiced living by a weekly rhythm for a while, feel free to make adjustments to create the rhythm that works best for you.

Here are the five things you'll need to do to set up your weekly rhythm:

Start with rest.
Plan your day of rest by the hour.
Unplug screens on your day of rest.
Assign a theme to each day of the week.
Defend the rhythm.

1. Start with Rest

Always start your weekly rhythm with Sabbath. A day of rest is God's weekly gift to you, to your spouse, and to your kids. Accept the gift. Make a plan. Then, rest.

We begin our week celebrating Shabbat, the Hebrew word for

Sabbath, on Friday night. If you attend church on a Sunday and you have children, you know Sunday is anything but a restful day, so pick a day you can actually rest. Your day of rest doesn't have to begin on an evening or on a Friday. Simply set aside a day—ideally a twenty-four-hour period—when you rest and do nothing else.

We begin with a Shabbat dinner, praying blessings over our kids and enjoying being together. Dinner is sometimes homemade and other times ordered in, nothing fancy. For us, the important part is being together without screens or other plans so we can tell stories, honor each family member, and process the week together.[2]

2. Plan Your Day of Rest by the Hour

If you're like me, the idea of planning a day of rest by the hour might feel exhausting in and of itself. But here's what I learned the hard way—if you don't work to plan out your day of rest, you'll work on your day of rest. It's that simple. Our day of rest is the most regimented day of the week, except for the summer when we spend our Saturdays on the lake swimming, eating, tubing, fishing, and eating some more.

For the rest of the year, we break our Sabbath day into roughly three-hour blocks of time. Although what we do in those blocks of time changes from one season to the next, there are some constants.

- *Alone time.* Both Josh and I have a three-hour block of alone time. While I have my alone time, Josh is spending time with the kids, and vice versa. I sometimes use my alone time to take a bath or read; Josh uses his alone time to go for a bike ride or to be in his workshop.

- *One-on-one dates with the kids.* We use another three-hour block to spend time with each of our three children. Josh might take Kennedy on a date to the creek to catch minnows while I stay with the two boys. When Josh returns, I go out with one of the boys. We try to fit in a date with each of the kids. If Kennedy didn't get her date with me on our Sabbath one week, it'll be her turn the next week. Right now, we're in a season where we can have our one-on-one dates with the oldest two while the youngest is napping. Be creative with your time.

- *Family activity.* We set aside a three-hour block to do something together, such as hiking, biking, board games, or brunch as a family.
- *Movie.* We end most of our Sabbath nights with popcorn and a family movie together snuggled on the couch.

Every family is different, so feel free to plan your day in larger or smaller blocks of time and to spend your time in ways that best serve the needs of your family. Consider it a trial-and-error exercise. You may not find a rhythm that feels completely restful in the first few months, especially if you have little kids. But don't beat yourselves up over it. Look back together at what worked and what didn't work, and readjust for the next week. We learned, for example, to use paper plates, prepare simple meals or eat leftovers (breakfast for dinner is always a huge win in our house), and commit to no house projects. The latter pulls us immediately back into our to-do list. The main point is to be intentional with the time so that you and every member of your family get what you need out of your day of rest. That's how you put the soul of your family center stage.

God has lavished you with a weekly gift of rest. Don't refuse it. Receive it for the beautiful gift it is. Imagine it as a seed you get each week, one you can plant in a family orchard. Sow the seed, water it, and watch the fruit of rest multiply in the life and atmosphere of your family.

3. Unplug Screens on Your Day of Rest

Turn your devices off and put them away—for the entire day.

I said what I said.

If you're already scrambling to defend all the reasons you can't possibly be separated from your phone, stop. I've heard or used most of those excuses myself. If you need your phone to take photos, get a small digital camera. If you want to be reachable in the event of an emergency, tell loved ones where you'll be and when you'll be back. You can also purchase an alternate phone with no apps. If you need your GPS, buy a paper atlas and teach your kids to use a map. The point is, our tendency is to keep justifying why we need to be on devices more than why we need to be off devices, and we all know that we need the latter.

4. Assign a Theme to Each Day of the Week

Kids need routine to thrive. This one simple exercise gives everyone in your home an idea of what's ahead each day. We do that by giving each day of the week a theme that reflects the purpose or focus of that day:

Ramp-Up Sunday
Motivating Monday
Tough Tuesday
Meeting Wednesday
Throwback Thursday
Fun Friday
Sabbath Saturday

We call Sunday Ramp-Up Sunday because it's the day we prepare for the week ahead. We start the day with church, come home for lunch, and spend the afternoon as a family cleaning the house and getting ready for the week to come. Each person is assigned to clean a specific part of the house that week and must fold their own laundry. Sunday is also one of our favorite days—clean sheet day! At dinner, Josh brings a calendar, and we walk through the week ahead so everyone knows what to expect in terms of work meetings, school schedules, activities, and fun events. I add my meal plan for the week as well.

Knowing the weekly schedule helps to calm anxiety in children who thrive on knowing what to expect. If Josh is unable to tuck the kids in bed because he's going to be out of town or has an evening work commitment, the kids have time to process their disappointment instead of it being sprung on them last minute.

The themes we assign to each day of the week also reflect the energy required for each day, starting with an ascent into a peak and then ending in a descent.

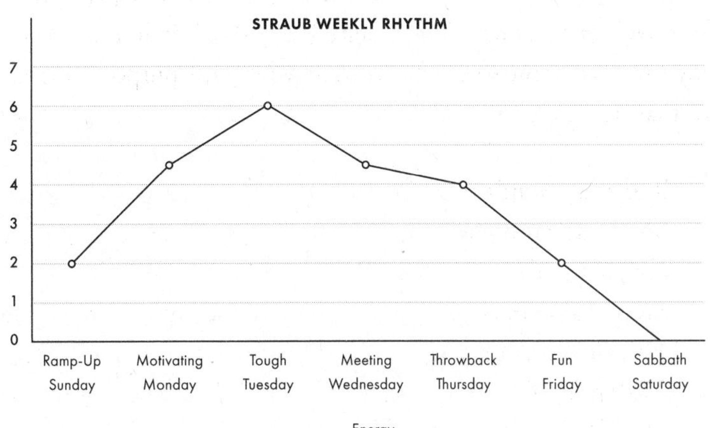

Motivating Monday is the first day of school and work. There's a reason the internet has more memes for Monday than any other day of the week—it takes some effort to get going. Josh also tries to schedule activities on Monday that require creativity and bring him energy so he's going into Tuesday feeling energized rather than drained. Since I schedule the kids' schoolwork and activities each day, I try to do the same. By Tough Tuesday, our family is firing on all cylinders. Tuesday is the day Josh works later than normal to get as much done early in the week as possible.

Meeting Wednesday isn't much different than Tough Tuesday except that Josh tries to quit work at a normal hour, if possible. We also keep Wednesdays, as much as we can, for online meetings and phone calls, or meetings I might have with friends and playdates for the kids.

By Throwback Thursday, our energy levels are beginning to come down into rest again. With a lot of moving parts Monday through Wednesday, Josh and I can feel a bit disconnected by Thursday. We try to use Thursday as our date night to throw back to what matters most, our relationship with each other. Josh tries to end work a little earlier to get more time with the kids before we head out for the evening.

We wind down on Fun Friday with either a day off tinkering around the house or with work projects and meetings that didn't get finished during the first four days. We end our week celebrating all the good we experienced that week during our Shabbat dinner Friday night and then enjoy our day of rest on Sabbath Saturday.[3]

Give every day of the week a purpose and make it work for you. Finding your family rhythm takes practice, trial and error, and ongoing communication. Our friends Blake and Chandler keep track of their week on a spreadsheet. Josh and I use a shared online calendar. At the end of the week, evaluate what worked well and what didn't so you can keep adjusting.

5. Defend the Rhythm

Once your rhythm is set, you can be sure that circumstances will try to interrupt it and knock you back into your old patterns of doing, working, and separating as a family on your day of rest. Military deployments, frequent work travel, family traditions, or other circumstances can make it difficult to not only develop a weekly rhythm but also keep it. This is why you want to create a rhythm that works for your family and then defend the rhythm.

Josh helps military families do this, especially when one parent is away on deployment. When Josh traveled a lot, I developed a woe-is-me mentality because I felt left alone. But my pitiful attitude left me directionless and had a negative impact on the atmosphere of our home, something we had to change. Now, whether or not Josh is out of town, we do everything we can to defend our rhythm of rest, even when we go on vacation or visit family for the holidays. We also invite others into our rhythm if we're out of town or have guests in our home. We find so many families are energized by it—a practice that spreads the movement of putting family center stage.

Set Your Daily Rhythms

Once you find a weekly rhythm that works for your family, move into planning your daily rhythms. When setting daily rhythms, continue to prioritize living from a mindset of rest by thinking of the day as beginning with dinner and getting a good night's sleep. Upon waking, rather than rushing into the day, start with something that brings you life. Pray or meditate and ask God what he was up to in your life while you slept. Surrender the day ahead into his care. Exercise. Make a gratitude list. Eat a healthy breakfast while sitting at the table rather than rushing around. Whatever you do, choose daily rhythms to help you live from rest, so when the dog tears up the house or the kids start bickering, you can handle it without losing your cool.

After starting with rest, develop a structure for the rest of your day. To structure his day, Josh uses four habits developed by Justin Whitmel Earley in his book *The Common Rule*. Justin's four daily habits of purpose include Scripture before phone, kneeling prayer three times a day, one meal with others, and one hour with the phone off.[4] We like to keep our phones off for the first hour of the day and the last hour before we fall asleep. We prioritize dinner together as a family every day and have a no-screen rule at mealtime.

Josh and I also prioritize exercise. We fight for each other to get time to work out because we show up for our family much better when we regularly move our bodies. Our daily schedule usually runs from about 5:30 a.m. to 9:00 p.m. Josh likes to work out first thing in the morning. I like to spend time alone praying. If we don't do these things before the kids are out of bed, they're unlikely to happen. I also set aside one day to run errands so I'm not frantic every other day of the week. Fight for what you need in each day of your week.

Celebrate. Celebrate. Celebrate.

Don't forget to add celebration to your rhythms. If God can stop each day and look back at what he created and call it good, then you can too. Celebrate a great school day, a finished work project, or a friend's recent accomplishment.

Make plans to create memories for the milestones: birthdays, the beginning and ending of the school year, success with an exercise program or eating regimen, or the completion of a degree or other major accomplishment. If your spouse usually runs with this, ask him or her how you can help with the celebration. For the impromptu celebrations and unexpected occasions, I keep a list of celebration ideas on my phone.

Make a list of ways you can celebrate the humans who live under your roof. What has your spouse accomplished or contributed to your life that merits recognition and validation? What about your kids? What gifts do they have that they don't see in themselves? How might you call out and celebrate those gifts in them?

As you think about ways to celebrate your loved ones, consider how you can make the most of smaller moments. We often celebrate by reading dinnertime blessings over each person, having movie dates at home, sitting around a campfire in the backyard, or the house favorite, holding an impromptu dance party with stage lights and microphones in our dining room. Dance parties have created moments that are forever woven into the celebration memories of the Straub home.

Finding those moments for your family comes by establishing rhythms your children will carry into theirs. Just as it is with money, if you don't tell your time where to go, you'll waste it. Rhythms are a beautiful cadence, a gift given to us by God to order our world, to work from rest and not for it, and to live a lifestyle of embracing the moments so we can celebrate—especially ten years from now when our kids have a decade of memories of being center stage.

15

DECISION 7: SET VALUES

How to See Your Family as a Verb, Not a Noun

JOSH

In any given dictionary, the word "family" is a noun. But nouns stand still. Your family does not. You move in one direction or another based on the values you adhere to, the actions you take, and the vision you set. Your family is a verb, moving in a direction. The question is, can you clearly see the direction your family is going?

Carlos and Rachel could not. They felt directionless. Both were working fifty-plus hours a week, not including their hour-long commutes, and their two kids spent every day of the week in daycare or with grandparents from morning until early evening. Rachel longed for more time with her kids, but she couldn't see how to get it. Carlos, a medical doctor just out of residency, worked long and irregular hours.

With their frantic pace taking its toll, they approached Christi and me to help them find a more manageable way of life. To start, we invited them to identify their family values. That's a process that often requires quite a bit of time, which is why I was taken aback at how fast and effortless it seemed to be for Carlos and Rachel to present their family values. When Carlos handed me the paper, I saw five values written across the top of the page: Faith. Family. Financial independence. Hospitality. Humor.

On the surface, they were resolved in what seemed like firm agreement on these five values. But the more they described their situation and began identifying action steps under each value, the more incongruity I noticed in their communication. An air of underlying resentment billowed to the surface, and it became clear that they weren't as unified as it appeared. So where was the kink in the hose, or the reason they reached out to us in the first place?

When we asked them to put action steps under each value, it was apparent that Rachel wanted to quit her job yesterday. She was ready to have more time at home with the kids. And it's not that Carlos didn't want that for her—he did. He just wasn't quite ready for it to happen yet. Carlos wanted to reach a level of financial independence first. Doing the values exercise revealed the disconnect. They held the same values; she just prioritized one value and he prioritized another.

There are consequences for how we choose to live our lives. If you value financial independence over family, you might get wealthier sooner, but at the consequence of missing out on the early years at home with your kids. If you value family over financial independence, you will get more time at home with your kids, but at the consequence of a having a smaller bank account earlier in life. The beauty, though, is you have authority over your life to decide! You just have to remain disciplined and resolved in who Team (your last name) is.

Being disciplined and resolved will sometimes require making hard decisions. I have turned down what I once considered dream jobs because when we assessed the opportunities in light of our family values, the jobs didn't measure up. At the same time, knowing that those jobs were a mismatch with our values made our decisions easier. We didn't have to agonize or make a list of pros and cons; we simply had to make the best decisions we could considering who Team Straub is and what's best for everybody. The same is true for you.

Why Set Values?

The word *value* means "something intrinsically desirable."[1]

Whether or not you realize it, you live by a set of values. Do an inventory of the last six months of your life. Look at your calendar. How did you spend your time? What activities did you prioritize? With whom did you spend the most time? And what did you spend the most time doing, especially when you weren't working?

Now look at your bank account. How did you spend your discretionary income? Did you prioritize material possessions, road trips, or home improvements? Is your money being invested in a retirement plan, education plan, or savings account? Each spending decision represents a value.

Where we spend our time and money tells us what we value—what we intrinsically desire in the here and now. And what we desire in the here and now moves our family in a particular direction. Invest in road trips today and you'll have memories and stories five years from now. Invest in home improvement and you'll have larger home equity five years from now. Invest in a retirement account and you'll have a bigger nest egg many years from now. None of these decisions are right or wrong. But what you intrinsically desire will take you in a particular direction with your finances and your family's way of life.

What Carlos intrinsically desired was financial freedom. What Rachel intrinsically desired was spending time with her kids. Carlos thought Rachel could get time with the kids after they had reached financial freedom (a future outlook on the value of family). Rachel didn't want to wait for financial freedom to get time with the kids (a present outlook on the value of family). The disconnect in how they prioritized their values left her feeling trapped in what she described as a "rat race."

Setting family values will only work for you if you listen to and communicate with your spouse. You need to agree on one set of values because two different visions and directions will split your family apart. Carlos and Rachel had to stop coaching and enter counseling to work through the resentment and discover the deeper reasons behind their individual values. Carlos grew up in poverty. Though he couldn't see it at the time, his strong desire to provide for his family financially left him not providing for them relationally. Rachel grew up in a divorced home and rarely got to see her mom, who had to work two and sometimes three jobs as a single parent. Their individual stories revealed the deeper narrative behind their intrinsically held values. Once Carlos and Rachel saw the other's reasoning, they were able to fight for each other and come up with a plan for the direction of their family—her working a part-time job closer to home until he had more stability in his job post residency.

Your family-rooted value system gives every individual in your family a safe place from which to launch and a safe place to which they can return as they discover their God-given purpose. As we say in our family, roots and wings. Values keep us rooted. They also give us wings to fly in the right direction so we can live with purpose.

Three Exercises for Setting Your Family Values

We walk families through three exercises to set their family values: discovery, values, and action steps. Discovery is the first exercise to help you see on paper what your family already values. The values exercise helps you identify your family values, and the action steps exercise helps you make a plan to live by them. Again, you probably already have a pretty good idea of what your family values are, but until you see everything on paper, you might not see them for what they are.

Invite your kids into these exercises. Setting values is putting your family—not just you or your marriage—center stage. Also, you don't have to fully complete the discovery exercise to begin setting your values. If you need to go back and keep working on the discovery exercise later, do that. Allow it to be a working document that helps guide the direction of your family.

As you complete the discovery exercise, you'll likely begin to see your family values come to life. Then move on to officially choosing and prioritizing your top five values. Once you have your values in place, you can identify action steps for living out those values and steering the direction of your family.

Exercise 1: Discovery

The objective of discovery is to help you document what brings your family to life so you can live from a spirit of abundance, gratitude, and purpose. Start by pulling together what you have already learned about your family by working through Decisions 1–6. You'll need a blank piece of paper or the downloadable Famous at Home worksheet.[2]

If using a blank piece of paper, fold it in half. You'll use the top half of the paper to focus on hobbies and family interests and the bottom half to document family mottoes and ways your family serves others. Start by writing the name of each person in your immediate family across the top of the page so you have a column for each person. Add a column for your family as well. Here is what that would look like for our family.

Josh	Christi	Landon	Kennedy	Micah	Family

Hobbies and Interests. Under each person's name, list up to three hobbies or interests that family member enjoys. What activity or passion brings each person to life? If you struggle to find time for hobbies in your current season of life, write down any hobbies you enjoyed when you were growing up. What passions did you give up or what interests just seemed to fade away as you became an adult? Write those down too. Where you see a family truly alive, you'll find adults who have rediscovered their inner child.

As kids, Christi and I both loved being on the water. But having young children meant we weren't doing much at all on the weekends. Our family value of adventure was difficult to live out in that season of life. When our kids got a little older, though, we decided to review our budget to see where we could reallocate money to live out our family value of adventure. At the time, we had someone cleaning our house every two weeks. With an intrinsic desire to raise resourceful kids and live a life of adventure, we reallocated funds to join a boat club. Today, we all pitch in to keep the house clean on Ramp-Up Sunday so we can spend as much time as possible on the lake.

Once you've documented everyone's individual hobbies, move to the family column. Write down the hobbies and activities you already do together as a family. What brings you to life as a family right now? Playing tennis? Going to amusement parks? Writing and singing music? What traditions do you want to carry into the next generation? Visiting baseball stadiums, art galleries, or museums? Weekly Shabbat meals? An annual family trip? Write them all down.

Mottoes and Service. Once you've documented your individual and family hobbies, use the bottom half of the page to write down your family mottoes and ways your family can serve others that bring you all to life. Create a chart with two columns.

Mottoes	**Service**

We all have family mottoes—phrases we say that define who we are and who we aren't.

"We tell the truth."
"We do hard things first."
"We treat others as we want to be treated."
"We bring solutions, not problems."

What three mottoes, phrases, or sayings does your family use to describe who you are? Write them down. Then write down three mottoes defining who your family is not.

"We don't whine or complain."
"We don't quit."
"We don't cheat."
"We don't tolerate bullying."

Once you've written down your mottoes, sit down with your family and talk about the ways you love to serve others. We love inviting other families into our boating adventures to give them a reprieve from their own busyness and to give us all an opportunity to connect more deeply with one another. You may also have your own individual ways you like to serve. Write them all down because each person's unique gifts can work together toward your family values. For example, if one of you loves cooking, another loves making people feel welcome, and another loves decorating, your family may very well be able to host others together with the value of hospitality. Write down the ways you love to serve and see what patterns emerge.

As you complete the discovery session, you might begin to see values jump off the pages from everything you wrote down. But you might not. The families we coach love completing the discovery exercise as a standalone because it enables them to discuss the why behind the activities they're involved in and what brings them to life. Our hope for you as you complete the discovery exercise is that it also brings a renewed energy and meaning to everything you say yes to as a family.[3]

Exercise 2: Values

Now that you've gathered information about what brings your family life and discussed who your family already is, you're ready to set your family values. Remember, the goal is to use your values to vector your family in a new direction, making a series of two-degree shifts, not a sharp ninety-degree turn. Sharp turns create a high probability of crashing and burning. Don't try to make your family something it's not. Instead, identify values that enable you to live in abundance, gratitude, and purpose. Don't stay in a cycle of doing what sucks the life out of your family.

Your objective is to set three to five values for your family. Any more than that and you'll likely end up directionless as a family with no set values. We have five family values guiding who we are: faith, family, adventure, connection, and purpose. These five values help us make decisions about where we live, how we work, where we vacation, when we prioritize rest, and how we approach our kids' education. Without our five values, I don't think we'd be leading Famous at Home today.

To find your three to five values, begin with the list of 100 Commonly Held Family Values on page 206. Individually, read through the list on your own first and circle the top ten values you most want to define your family. If you're a solo parent with older kids, invite them into the process as well.

Now, rank your circled values from one to ten in importance—one for the value that's your highest priority and ten for the value that's your lowest priority. Once you and your spouse or you and your kids have your individual top ten in rank order, come together and narrow your list to no fewer than three and no more than five values. A great place to start is with the values that made the cut on everyone's list. What values did all of you pick? Start there.

If you have Bible verses you live by, you could also begin to

100 COMMONLY HELD FAMILY VALUES

Acceptance
Accomplishment
Achievement
Adaptability
Adventure
Affluence
Altruism
Ambition
Assertiveness
Beauty
Bravery
Commitment
Compassion
Confidence
Contentment
Conviction
Courage
Creativity
Curiosity
Dependability
Depth
Dignity
Discipline
Duty
Emotional safety
Empathy
Encouragement
Excellence
Fairness
Faith
Faithfulness
Family
Fearlessness
Financial independence
Flexibility
Focus
Freedom
Friendliness
Generosity
Gentleness
Goodness
Grace
Gratitude
Health
Holiness
Honesty
Honor
Hopefulness
Hospitality
Humility
Humor
Imagination
Independence
Influence
Integrity
Intelligence
Intentionality
Intimacy
Joy
Justice
Kindness
Knowledge
Leadership
Love
Loyalty
Marriage
Maturity
Mindfulness
Obedience
Optimism
Organization
Passion
Patience
Peace
Perseverance
Philanthropy
Presence
Professionalism
Prudence
Purpose
Resilience
Resolve
Respect
Responsibility
Righteousness
Sacrifice
Security
Self-control
Sincerity
Spontaneity
Stability
Success
Sympathy
Trustworthiness
Understanding
Vision
Vulnerability
Whimsy
Wisdom
Wonder

identify your values that way. Is there a value the verse speaks to? Or you could do it in reverse, applying a Bible verse to your newly established values. Again, this is all about what makes your family unique. Who has God called your family to be?

Values give your family identity. They also guide your family purpose. Once you have your three to five values, post them somewhere. Put them on a plaque or create some wall art and display them so you can talk about them with your kids and even visitors who come by.

Exercise 3: Action Steps

Once you set your values, the goal is to live by them. We coach families to identify three to four action steps for each value. The actions you identify will be a guide to lead your family toward the values you want to live by. To capture your action steps, you can use a large piece of paper or a poster board, or you can print out the downloadable worksheet.[4] If you're using a piece of paper or poster board, draw a chart that looks like the one on the following page.

Use the first column to write in the three to five values you set. Use the remaining columns to document your action steps for each value.

For our family value of adventure, we go to the lake (weather permitting) at least once a week between May and September. When Matt and Vanessa set their family values, they included the value of hospitality. One of their hospitality action steps is hosting another family in their home for dinner at least once a week. Dan and Maria, another couple we coached, act on their value of faith by attending church three times a month and rotating as leaders in their small group for six months of the year. They devote the other six months to recharging their family (going on date nights or family outings) and serving as God leads them (bringing dinner

Value	Daily Action Step	Weekly Action Step	Monthly Action Step	Yearly Action Step

to a neighbor in need or serving at a homeless shelter). Our friends Josh and Nicole act on their value of health by working out five days a week, eating meat only one meal a week, and attending individual therapy two times a month.

When you set action steps, make them doable, measurable, adjustable, and part of your LIFEstyle.

Doable. As a general rule, we coach families to set at least one daily action step, one weekly action step, and one monthly action step. You can add a yearly action step as well. A daily, weekly, and monthly rhythm for each value is much easier to remember than too many action steps. And remember, you want these values to become a lifestyle, to fit into the rhythms of your life together. Therefore, like any other goal, you want to make your action steps doable. You don't need another thing in your life to feel unnecessarily guilty about.

If you can't live up to the action steps you set, go back and review them to make them doable. For example, Matt and Vanessa initially wanted to have people over two nights a week, but with their kids' activities and their own work schedules, that wasn't doable, so they had to adjust. Dan and Maria had a difficult time leading a monthly small group all year long and still finding time for their marriage. As part of living out their value of faith, they chose a more doable schedule of leading small group half the year so they could focus more intentionally on recharging their family the other half of the year.

Measurable. If your action steps aren't measurable, how will you know whether you lived them out? For example, if joy is a value, a general action item might be, "We will hold family dance parties." But a measurable action item would set specific criteria: "We will hold family dance parties three times a month, inviting another family to join us once a month."

Adjustable. In his book *The Three Big Questions for a Frantic Family*, Patrick Lencioni suggests sitting down together every month and assessing action steps by marking them green (crushing it), yellow (doing okay), or red (haven't done it). Though some of the families we coach find this helpful, others find it laborious. Whatever method you choose to track your action steps, make sure they work for your family. I like Lencioni's green, yellow, and red approach because if we have a red action step too many months in a row, we know it's time to adjust either the action step or the value itself. As our children get older, we find ourselves adjusting our action steps each year. In the past year, we even adjusted two of our family values.

LIFEstyle. Set a once-a-month or once-a-quarter family meeting to review your LIFEstyle. The word *LIFE* is in capital letters for a reason. You want your values to reinforce and support the rhythms you set in Decision 6: Establish Family Rhythms. If your values do not bring life to your family or a spirit of peace to the environment of your home, make some adjustments.

Many of the couples I coach choose family as a value but neglect to identify any action steps for cultivating their marriage. If you are a few months along in living your values and realize you overlooked your marriage, go back and adjust. Add 15 Minutes a Day as a daily action step or a date night as a weekly one. Find what brings life to your marriage and make it a lifestyle.

When it comes to our family rhythms, we allow our three children to participate in only one activity at a time. Two activities at a time for any given child leaves our family running ragged and interrupts the flow of relationship and peace in our home. We also see many families serving on Sunday morning at their church, leading a small group during the week, and attending a midweek service, yet they constantly feel exhausted and have no actual time for their family. The question I ask these families is, "Are you serving out of a feeling of guilt or a sense of conviction?" There is a season for every purpose under heaven, and Jesus came to bring us life. If your family lifestyle is becoming a deathstyle, make adjustments.

Decide for Life

We live in a world that competes for our time, attention, and identity. If we don't stop to evaluate the decisions we make, we'll find ourselves not living from the fullness of the life God has for us but feeling stuck, frustrated, and perhaps in a directionless or lifeless marriage.

The culture around you is not designed to support your family. You are the only one looking out for them. And every decision you make supports another.

When you decide to change your mindset in just one area of your life, you change your family atmosphere.

When you decide to change your family atmosphere, everyone feels safer to talk about emotions.

When you decide to talk about emotions, you're better able to listen to your spouse's heart.

When you decide to listen to your spouse's heart, you learn how to enter a loved one's world.

When you decide to enter your child's world, you learn how to champion their heart.

When you decide to establish family rhythms, your family lives from rest.

When you decide to set values, your family lives on purpose.

Do you see how all of these decisions are verbs, how they move your family in one direction or another? How every decision is doable, actionable, and not adding anything to your already busy day? Sure, setting rhythms and values will take some time, but even the process of deciding to create rhythms and values helps you get 15 Minutes a Day with your spouse and 20 Minutes a Day entering your child's world.

Again, fast-forward a decade or two, or maybe three. Imagine sitting on your back porch watching your grandchildren run around the yard. Looking back on your life, what will have mattered? The Bible says, "Grandchildren are the crowning glory of the aged" (Proverbs 17:6). Though some days will feel more difficult than others, don't take your eyes off the "crowning glory" of the generations ahead. Living with intentionality and purpose is not an impossible dream. By putting your family center stage every day, one decision at a time, you not only get to set the direction your family is moving, you also get to live out your family's God-given mission for his Kingdom.

16

THE POWER OF SHOWING UP: YOUR FAMILY MISSION

JOSH

When asked to identify the most important commandment in all of Scripture, "Jesus replied, 'You must love the LORD your God with all your heart, all your soul, and all your mind.' This is the first and greatest commandment. A second is equally important: 'Love your neighbor as yourself'" (Matthew 22:37-39).

In two sentences, Jesus narrowed his entire mission to one word: love. We can discuss the fruit of the Spirit (Galatians 5:22-23), the Ten Commandments (Exodus 20:3-17), or every definition of love mentioned throughout the Bible, but to know Jesus is to know love. He is love. He embodies love. Love is his nature.

One of the ways to live out your family values is to develop your family mission—to find what makes your family greater than the sum of its parts. Though it might sound like a formality or something that doesn't have much impact on your day-to-day life, your family mission holds a much bigger purpose. Your family mission could very well be what holds your family together in the hardest seasons you face, just as it did for Matt and Vanessa.

A month after Matt and Vanessa finished their marriage coaching, Vanessa was hit by a drunk driver in a terrible car accident. For the next year, Matt had to become a full-time caregiver to their three kids, including a newborn, and to Vanessa until she was back on her feet again. "Had we not had the coaching tools to communicate and the values in place for our family, I'm not sure we would've made it through that accident together," Matt later told me.

The grace and perseverance Matt and Vanessa embodied throughout this ordeal inspired everyone around them. Matt and the kids owned their family value of hospitality as they cared for Vanessa. And the joy—oh, the joy! That was another one of their family values. Had you gone to their house to help them during that challenging season, you would most certainly have left with a smile, taking some of their joy home along with you. That was the atmosphere Matt and Vanessa cultivated in their home. They carried it with them wherever they went. They lived out their values.

Think about the families you admire and respect. You witness them from afar and either want to hang out with them or want to be like them—not because of their money, jobs, or social standing, but because of how they live, the way they care for one another, and how they all show up to serve others. You love how you feel after spending time with them. These families don't announce their mission and values. But when you are with them, you know they embody something different from what the rest of the world has to offer.

Matt and Vanessa embodied hospitality and joy, even in their worst moments as a family. As they lived out their mission of "spreading joy through hospitality," not only were their lives changed, the lives of those around them were changed as well.

That's the hope of this book—for the Seven Decisions to not just change your family but also inspire the world around you. That's what it means to have a family mission.

Establishing Your Family Mission

To be intentional about living out your purpose as a family, it's helpful to have a family mission. Your mission is how you hope to influence others as a family. Your mission is comprised of three components: your name, your values/purpose/motto, and how you live it out.

Here's a phrase you can use to help develop your mission. Use it as a template to start, but then make it your own.

> The [*last name*] family mission is to [*values/purpose/motto*] by [*how we live it out*].

Here is how we used the template to develop our family mission:

> The *Straub* family mission is to *bring the hope and joy of God's Kingdom to earth* by *inviting families into experiences that cultivate intentional connection, life-giving adventure, and Spirit-weaved purpose.*

And here is how Matt and Vanessa wrote their mission:

> The *Jackson* family mission is to *show hospitality to everyone, especially strangers,* by *inviting others into our home for meals, engaging in laughter and games, and teaching our kids to serve others first.*

To make it memorable, we shorten our mission to "bringing life to families through experience and adventure." Matt and Vanessa shortened theirs to "spreading joy through hospitality."

Jesus narrowed his mission to one word: "love."

You can do that too if you'd like. What one word defines your family? Start with your longer phrase and narrow it down. Make this exercise your own. And do whatever you can to make your mission memorable.

To start, identify a Bible verse or family motto your family embodies. For example:

"Love your neighbor as yourself."
"Treat others as you want to be treated."
"Show hospitality to strangers."
"Work hard. Play hard."

Now pull out the values you identified in the previous chapter and look them over. What one or two words best describe your family? If you have trouble, think about what you've heard other people say about your family, which may or may not be one of your values. For example:

Humorous
Joyful
Inspiring
Hospitable

People have sometimes described our family as "caring" and "genuine." Though these are not our values, these adjectives complement our family values of connection and purpose.

Finally, in what ways does your family live out your motto?

If you haven't yet taken action steps to live this out, no worries. The point of defining your family mission is to know what you're walking toward—becoming a family that influences the culture more than the culture influences you. Then you'll know how best to serve others from the core of who you are. Here are some examples of how other families live out their motto and influence others:

"Coach and serve in a local sports team/league."
"Feed the homeless."
"Run a retreat center."
"Own a restaurant together to serve our community."
"Sell produce at the local farmers market."

How does your family influence others? By participating in local youth leagues, caring for those in need, or showering others with fresh vegetables every weekend as you build your family produce business?

Take time as a family to pray through your mission for a few days. Use your dinner conversations to talk about what you embody as a family and to identify ways you can carry out your mission together. Just as with your values, how you carry out your family mission may evolve over time as your kids grow up and their passions and giftings become apparent. That's certainly been true for us.

The Hidden Blessing of Fame

You may have picked up this book with the intent of learning how to be celebrated as a parent or spouse. The object of fame, at least the pursuit of it, is about us. We want to be known and celebrated. But if in our pursuit of fame we continue making everyone else's story about us, we might be famous (for all the wrong reasons) but not celebrated.

When you begin applying the Seven Decisions, you'll be taking the journey from self-awareness (Decisions 1–3) to others-awareness (Decisions 3–5), and then to a purpose bigger than yourself (Decisions 6–7). Sure, the journey starts with you thinking of yourself, but the goal is that it ends with you thinking of yourself less and less.

In describing C. S. Lewis's perspective on humility, author and pastor Tim Keller writes, "If we were to meet a truly humble person . . . we would never come away from meeting them thinking they were humble. . . . The thing we would remember from meeting a truly gospel-humble person is how much they seemed to be totally interested in us. Because the essence of gospel-humility is not thinking more of myself or thinking less of myself, it is thinking of myself less."[1]

Therein lies the hidden blessing of being famous at home—the privilege of showing up in the world of another human being to set them free with the gift of love.

The Reward of Showing Up

Showing up is an art.

Showing up may mean choosing to attend your son's basketball game rather than staying late to help your team finish a big project at work. Or it may mean staying at work late to help your team instead of going to your son's basketball game.

The more you practice the Seven Decisions, the easier showing up becomes. Will you sometimes get it wrong? Yes, of course you will. But most of the time, your gut, or the Holy Spirit, will already be telling you what you need to do.

Showing up is taking the initiative to plan the anniversary getaway your spouse has been dreaming of.

Showing up is having the difficult conversation with your mom for overstepping her boundaries with your spouse.

Showing up is no longer allowing the elephant in the room to stifle communication in your marriage, and instead talking to your spouse about it.

Showing up is taking your family out fishing for the evening.

Showing up is surprising your kids for lunch at school.

Showing up is sending your family a silly video text or doing a FaceTime call while you travel away from home.

Showing up is mailing a gift to a friend.

Showing up is attending the funeral of a loved one.

Showing up is going to therapy for your own trauma.

Showing up is choosing the salad over the hamburger.

Showing up is deciding to prioritize your family for the holidays and not just do what you do every year because it's what you do every year.

Showing up happens with values to live by. A mission to live for. A purpose bigger than your family.

When you decide to turn your focus away from the chase and toward the hearts of those inside your home, the blessing of God in your family lineage continues to the thousandth generation.

Your family mission has the power to shape eternity.

Famous at Home

In 2014, during one of the most trying seasons for our family, I was sitting with my dad in the ICU about a week after his first heart-pump surgery. It was one of his first days of being able to sit up in a chair.

"Josh," he said, "when I was first diagnosed with congestive heart failure, I asked God to allow me to see you kids grow up. Now I'm asking him for a bonus, to enjoy my grandkids."

Little did we know the next two years would be filled with blood clots, long hospital stays, and three heart-pump surgeries. Yes, three pumps. Three times he had his chest opened. Three times he went to rehab. Watching him persevere was the proudest and saddest I ever felt. He lived in pain every day, fighting for his family.

But in the middle of the physical pain, God was answering my prayers for my dad. He confided in me about encounters he'd had on the operating table with loved ones who had preceded him in death. His body was failing, but his soul was enlivened. The frequency of our conversations about faith began to eclipse our lifelong conversations about sports. For those two years and through multiple surgeries, he held a wooden cross in his hand, becoming affectionately known by the nurses and doctors as the man who carried the cross.

As he fought to stay alive for his family for so many years, my dad's faith in what was to come started to occupy his every waking thought.

On November 5, 2016, Dad walked into the arms of Jesus. Holding his hand, reading Romans 8, and praying him into heaven was one of the most bittersweet moments of my life.

Having a PhD and a seminary degree didn't make my understanding of heaven any clearer than that of the next person. In the months following my dad's death, my mind often wandered to what my dad might be doing, who he's with, and what he knows.

Part of my grief process was to find out. I devoured books about heaven. I wanted a glimpse of hope in the midst of my tears. One of the greatest gifts of studying heaven was giving myself permission to dream about what it will be like when we reunite with our loved ones. When my dad gets to hold his grandkids in his arms. When the whole family gets to play baseball in the backyard.

It was during this season that I received Pastor Aaron's prophetic words that an angel had been sent to protect me in ways my dad wanted to but couldn't while he was alive. Later that same afternoon, I stood in our friends' kitchen with Aaron, telling him more about my dad and the story of the wooden cross. As I prepared to show Aaron a picture of that cross, which we'd had engraved on Dad's tombstone, Aaron stopped me.

"Wait," Aaron said, "I'll be right back." Aaron was visiting from out of town, and he ran upstairs to the guest room in our friends' home. When he came back down, he handed me a wooden cross. "Did it look like this?" he asked.

Once more, I teared up.

"Josh, I'm telling you, I never travel with this," Pastor Aaron said. "But the Holy Spirit told me to bring it. I even debated with him as I was heading out the door because, Lord knows, I didn't need to bring anything else on the plane. But now I know why he told me to bring it.

"Here," he said, handing it to me, "this is for you."

Since we had buried Dad's cross with him, I no longer had it. But now God was using Pastor Aaron to give me a cross just like the one Dad carried.

In his book *Sacred Fire,* Ronald Rolheiser wrote,

> Like Jesus, we can really send our spirits only after we go away.
>
> We experience this everywhere we go in life: a grown child has to leave home before her parents can fully understand and appreciate her for who she is. There comes a day in a young person's life when she stands

> before her parents and, in whatever way she articulates it, says the words: "It is better for you that I go away! Unless I go, you will never really know who I am. You will have some heartache now, but that pain will eventually become warm because I will come back to you in a deeper way."[2]

I believe this is what happened when my dad died—he came back to us in a deeper way. Through his death, he left us with a vision for the resurrection, one we continue to imagine and seek to impart to our children to this day. Our family mission is about partnering with Jesus in "bringing his Kingdom to earth." The new earth. In the words of my friend and pastor Rich Villodas, "The Bible doesn't end with souls ascending to a disembodied heaven. It ends with a fully embodied heaven descending to earth."[3]

This is why what we embody as a family matters. Because when we're eighty years old and sitting on our rocking chairs looking back on the kids we got to raise, one of the most powerful blessings we'll experience is knowing that being famous was never really about us.

JOIN US ON THE JOURNEY!

Living the Seven Decisions takes time. In many cases, doing so requires therapy, coaching, or outside consulting. If you have any questions about your journey or would like more information on upcoming events and coaching programs, such as our Leader's Heart Cohort, visit us at www.famousathome.com.

If you'd like to have Josh or someone from the Famous at Home team speak at your event or help you implement a family-friendly, emotionally intelligent culture into your organization or workplace, simply fill out the contact form at www.famousathome.com/contact.

We'd also love to hear from you. If you have a story of how the Seven Decisions helped your family, you can write to us at www.famousathome.com/contact or use #famousathomebook to share about it with others.

Thank you for allowing us to walk alongside you on your journey.

DISCUSSION QUESTIONS

1. The concept of being "famous at home" is central to this book. Who was "famous" for you when you were a child? Describe one person who was always there for you. How did his or her support encourage you and give you confidence? As you look at your own family, where do you see yourself already showing up for your spouse and kids, and where would you like to improve? How do you think your spouse and kids would answer this same question?

2. In chapter 2, Christi talks about chasing significance and affirmation, while Josh chased security through taking care of others. What do you chase in an attempt to prove your own worth? How does this pull you away from the important things in your life or prevent you from showing up for your family? How can living from your identity as a child of God help you live differently?

3. In chapter 3, Christi mentions that the way we spend our time, money, and mental energy (including screen time and social media) reveals our true priorities. Do you see a disconnect between what you *say* is most important to you and what you *actually* spend your time on? How would

you like to adjust your priorities, especially knowing that your children are always watching you? How can setting meaningful priorities help us positively influence those we love?

4. In John 5, Jesus asks a paralyzed man, "Would you like to get well?" Does this question hit home to you as you consider making changes in your family? What is holding you back from being willing to put in the work and make changes in your parenting and marriage? How can we move past the tendency to blame our spouses for the problems in our marriages?
5. In chapter 7, the authors point out that staying emotionally connected even in disagreement is one of the greatest predictors of a marriage's longevity. What is one way we can turn our hearts toward each other even when we don't see eye-to-eye? Describe a time when your spouse cheered you on, acting as your fan rather than as your opponent. What did that mean to you? How can experiences like this strengthen your relationship?
6. In chapter 8, Josh talks about how our attempts to change another person almost always end in failure. Can you remember a time when someone else tried to modify your behavior—whether that was your spouse, a child, a boss, your own parent, or someone else? How successful were they? How might your parenting look different if you focused less on changing your child's behavior and more on yourself and the person you're becoming?
7. In chapter 9, the authors use the illustration of a plane changing its trajectory by making small adjustments over

time. Does this image make change feel more possible for you as you think about what direction you want to go as a family? Christi then talks about changing a mindset through a few steps: identifying your primary pain point, coming up with a goal, and then adjusting one rhythm to help you meet that goal. How does breaking down the change process into these steps make it more accessible? What goal and rhythm would you like to set to help change the trajectory of your family and show up as the best version of you?

8. One way to change the atmosphere in your home, as discussed in chapter 10, is to spend more dedicated time in prayer for and with your family. What part does prayer play in your family? What are some ways you could more meaningfully pray for your spouse or children? Imagine the family prayer life you would like to have. What could help you become more comfortable praying together?

9. How were emotions handled in your family as you grew up? In chapter 11, Josh tells the story about Kennedy acting out until Christi helped her name her emotions—which unlocked the story of her tough afternoon. Have you ever experienced something similar with your spouse or children, where their behavior didn't make sense until you understood the emotion behind it? Why does being able to name our emotions help us move forward and respond to our circumstances in a healthier way? What steps could you take to help your family become more comfortable naming and expressing emotions?

10. Reflect on the practices of 15 Minutes a Day (setting aside time with your spouse to talk about the emotions you experienced that day) and 20 Minutes a Day (entering your

child's world and doing something he or she loves). What elements are already present in your family, and what seems new or challenging? How do you think implementing these practices might help you connect more deeply with your spouse or kids?

11. In chapter 14, Christi talks about implementing daily or weekly rhythms that encompass things like chores, schoolwork, exercise, devotions, family activities, and rest. What rhythms would be helpful to your family? Why is the idea of taking a day of rest so difficult for us to put into practice? If you were planning a day of rest for your family, what elements would you incorporate? What benefits do you think you would experience?

12. The final chapters of the book talk about developing your family values and mission. What excites you about this? What values jumped out at you as you read the list of 100 Commonly Held Family Values? How can having an established family mission statement give you a stronger sense of purpose? Share the kind of influence you hope to have on others as you, your spouse, and your children work together in God's Kingdom.

ACKNOWLEDGMENTS

In an ideal world, our acknowledgments would be more than words written on a page. They'd be a series of parties to celebrate each person individually—those who gave their time, effort, and talents to make this book a reality; those who selflessly helped us shape our own family story; and those who trusted us to walk alongside them to shape theirs. Even though we can't throw a dozen parties, we do want to acknowledge the contributions that made this book possible. Consider it a virtual dance party!

First, to our heavenly Father—may you be honored in our words and our lives. You are our joy, our foundation, our hope, and our first love. All of this is for you.

To Team Straub—Landon, Kennedy, and Micah—thank you for your input, patience, and support of Mum and Dad as we worked on this book. We love creating a life of adventure with you.

To Team Famous at Home, beginning with Janae Torgeson—none of this would be possible without you. Thank you for the way you love our family and serve Famous at Home (FAH). We love you! Jane Butler, your ideas, graphics, and insights bring FAH to life. Working with you has been a dream come true. Pastor Aaron, your prayers and friendship are priceless. Bill and Laurie Lokey, you spur us on, sharpen us and teach us daily. Thank you for your investment in us and the families of FAH.

To our FAH and Team Straub prayer team—you have covered us and invested so much time and love on our behalf. We are forever grateful to each of you. Your work for the Kingdom echoes into eternity.

To Bryan Norman, you have journeyed with us for eight years now, not just as our literary agent but also as our friend. Time flies when you're having fun! Thank you for your continued support and turning our desire to influence more families into a reality.

To the Tyndale team, you are such a joy to work with! Jon Farrar, thank you for believing in us and the message of *Famous at Home* from the very beginning. This book is a reality because of your support and vision for it. A special thanks to Dean, Christina, Sarah, Kristen, and your entire teams for the work and ideas you put into this book. Your gifts and talents are evident.

To Christine Anderson, our editor. Wow! What a beautiful and hard-working adventure we had together. Words cannot describe what a joy it was working with you. You not only made this book readable, but you also taught us so much about writing along the way. One of the blessings of this book was gaining your friendship.

To those mentioned throughout the book who have invested in our family through therapy, spiritual direction, coaching, or longtime friendship, we wouldn't be who we are today without you.

And to those we have had the privilege of coaching, or who have attended the Leader's Heart Cohort, your courage and commitment to living wholeheartedly and being famous at home is what brings us so much joy. *You* make what we do so rewarding as we all together multiply what it means to be famous at home. We love each and every one of you!

And saving the best for last, to our parents, Ray and Lora Lee Wood, and Mike and Sharon Hess—thank you for always loving us the way you do, living lives of integrity, and being the best grandparents our kids could ask for. And in honor of David Straub, we await the day of our resurrected reunion together.

NOTES

1. BEING FAMOUS

1. Jean M. Twenge, "Increases in Depression, Self-Harm, and Suicide Among U.S. Adolescents after 2012 and Links to Technology Use: Possible Mechanisms," *Psychiatric Research and Clinical Practice* 2, no. 1 (Summer 2020): 19–25, https://doi.org/10.1176/appi.prcp.20190015.
2. "John 13:33," *Pulpit Commentary*, Bible Hub, https://biblehub.com/commentaries/pulpit/john/13.htm.
3. W. E. Vine, *Vine's Expository Dictionary of New Testament Words*, s.v. "Know, Known, Knowledge, Unknown," https://www.studylight.org/dictionaries/eng/ved/k/know-known-knowledge-unknown.html.
4. *Strong's Concordance* definition, Interlinear Passage Lookup, Ephesians 3:19, s. v. "Know," https://www.studylight.org/study-desk/interlinear.html?q1=Ephesians+3:19.

3. YOUR BIGGEST FANS

1. Portions of this story adapted from Christi Straub, "Joy Comes in the Morning," *Eden & Vine*, Spring/Summer 2020, 56–61.
2. See tables of findings in Mario Mikulincer and Phillip R. Shaver, *Attachment in Adulthood: Structure, Dynamics, and Change* (New York: Guilford Publications, 2016), 155–160, 196, 201, 309–311, 313; see also Kim Leon and Deborah B. Jacobvitz, "Relationships Between Adult Attachment Representations and Family Ritual Quality: A Prospective, Longitudinal Study," *Family Process* 42, no. 3 (August 2004): 419–432, https://doi.org/10.1111/j.1545-5300.2003.00419.x.

4. YOUR BIGGEST ADVERSARY

1. "Habbakuk 2," *Pulpit Commentary*, Bible Hub, https://biblehub.com/commentaries/pulpit/habakkuk/2.htm.
2. Portions of this story adapted from Christi Straub, "Watchwomen: Standing Guard Over Your Marriage and Children," *Eden & Vine*, Fall/Winter 2021, 29–31.
3. Authors Stephen James and David Thomas talk about this same dynamic as it relates to boys in their book *Wild Things: The Art of Nurturing Boys* (Carol Stream, IL: Tyndale, 2009).

5. YOUR SIGNIFICANCE

1. Dale L. Mast, *And David Perceived He Was King* (Maitland, FL: Xulon Press, 2015), xxiii.

6. ARE YOU WILLING?

1. To learn more about the scope and demographics of this research, see David D. Burns, *Feeling Good Together: The Secret to Making Troubled Relationships Work* (New York: Broadway Books, 2008), 55–59.
2. Burns, *Feeling Good Together*, 58.
3. Burns, *Feeling Good Together*, 58.
4. Burns, *Feeling Good Together*, 60.
5. Burns, *Feeling Good Together*, 47–49.
6. Burns, *Feeling Good Together*, 58–59.
7. Burns, *Feeling Good Together*, 60.
8. Christi and I also pray the "Daily Prayer of Freedom" found in John Eldredge's book *Moving Mountains*. We recommend this book to couples who want to learn more about how to use prayer to engage in spiritual warfare on behalf of their families.

7. WHAT ARE YOU FIGHTING FOR?

1. This oft-quoted statement has been attributed to various sources.
2. John M. Gottman, *The Marriage Clinic: A Scientifically Based Marital Therapy* (New York: W.W. Norton, 1999), 24, 48, 106; John Mordechai Gottman, *What Predicts Divorce? The Relationship between Marital Processes and Marital Outcomes* (Hillsdale, NJ: Lawrence Erlbaum Associates, 1994).
3. We are grateful to Sue Johnson, Les Greenberg, and their colleagues for this powerful insight, which comes from their research in Emotionally Focused Therapy (EFT). To learn more about EFT research, visit the website of the International Centre for Excellence in Emotionally Focused Therapy (ICEEFT) at https://iceeft.com/eft-research-2/.
4. Burns, *Feeling Good Together*, 73.

5. John Gottman and Nan Silver, *What Makes Love Last? How to Build Trust and Avoid Betrayal* (New York: Simon and Schuster, 2012), xvii.
6. Gottman and Silver, *What Makes Love Last?,* 49.

8. WHO ARE YOU BECOMING?

1. "Parenting," *Oxford English Dictionary*, Lexico, https://www.lexico.com/en/definition/parenting.
2. "Becoming," *Oxford English Dictionary*, Lexico, https://www.lexico.com/en/definition/becoming.
3. Brené Brown, *Daring Greatly: How the Courage to be Vulnerable Transforms the Way We Live, Love, Parent, and Lead* (New York: Avery, 2012), 214.
4. Robert Epstein, "What Makes a Good Parent? A Scientific Analysis Ranks the 10 Most Effective Child-Rearing Practices," *Journal of Lifelong Faith* 5.3 (Fall 2011): 3–7, https://www.lifelongfaith.com/uploads/5/1/6/4/5164069/lifelong_faith_journal_5.3.pdf.
5. Epstein, "What Makes a Good Parent?," 4.

9. DECISION 1: CHANGE YOUR MINDSET

1. The point is not that kids shouldn't participate in activities, but that the activities should serve your kids and your family. If you or your child feel pressured into an activity, that's a red flag. We're huge fans of sports for child development and character building. But when child sports and the cultural mindset around success and identity are adding more stress to your family, fragmenting your family, or when you're more invested in the sport/activity than your child, it's time to reevaluate why you're doing it.
2. John Gottman and Julie S. Gottman, *Emotion Coaching: The Heart of Parenting DVD and Parenting Workbook* (Seattle, WA: Gottman Institute, 2013). For more information, see www.gottman.com/shop/emotion-coaching-video-series.

10. DECISION 2: CHANGE YOUR ATMOSPHERE

1. "Atmosphere," *Cambridge Dictionary*, https://dictionary.cambridge.org/dictionary/english/atmosphere.
2. "Hagios," *Strong's Concordance*, Bible Hub, https://www.biblehub.com/greek/40.htm.

11. DECISION 3: TALK ABOUT EMOTIONS

1. These brain functions are more fully described from a parenting perspective in Daniel J. Siegel and Tina Payne Bryson, *The Whole-Brain Child: Twelve Revolutionary Strategies to Nurture Your Child's Developing*

Mind (New York: Delacorte Press, 2011); and from a clinical perspective in Daniel J. Siegel, *Pocket Guide to Interpersonal Neurobiology: An Integrative Handbook of the Mind* (New York: Norton, 2012). I also explain these neurobiological processes in my book *Safe House: How Emotional Safety Is the Key to Raising Kids Who Live, Love, and Lead Well* (New York: Waterbrook, 2015).

2. Siegel and Bryson, *The Whole-Brain Child*, 38–41.
3. Siegel, *Pocket Guide to Interpersonal Neurobiology*, 20–21.
4. Daniel J. Siegel, *Mindsight: The New Science of Personal Transformation* (New York: Random House, 2010), 137–139.
5. Straub, *Safe House*, 41–43.
6. "Epieikeia," *Strong's Concordance and HELPS Word-Studies*, Bible Hub, https://biblehub.com/greek/1932.htm.
7. "Philippians 4," *Pulpit Commentary*, Bible Hub, https://biblehub.com/philippians/4-5.htm
8. "The meek," *Vincent's Word Studies*, Bible Hub, https://biblehub.com/commentaries/matthew/5-5.htm.
9. Gottman and Gottman, *Emotion Coaching*.

12. DECISION 4: LISTEN TO YOUR SPOUSE'S HEART

1. When both of you are in survival mode, one of the strategies you can use is to agree on a code word to let your spouse know you need a few minutes to regroup. Making it a funny word or phrase such as "smelly toes" can also be a way to jolt you both out of the offense for a few minutes to gather your thoughts. Use one of your 15 Minutes a Day conversations to identify a code word and to discuss what you need from one another in order to feel safe when these reactive moments strike.
2. For a more in-depth analysis on this, we highly recommend David D. Burns's book *Feeling Good Together: The Secret to Making Troubled Relationships Work* (New York: Broadway Books, 2008), 65–69.
3. Burns describes these strategies along with a few others in *Feeling Good Together*, 98.

13. DECISION 5: ENTER YOUR CHILD'S WORLD

1. This idea of playing on the floor is based on forty years of child development research by Stanley Greenspan. He developed a method of child therapy called floortime. You can learn about this technique and more in Stanley Greenspan with Nancy Breslau Lewis, *Building Healthy Minds: The Six Experiences that Create Intelligence and Emotional Growth in Babies and Children* (Boston: Da Capo Press, 1999).
2. Greenspan and Lewis, *Building Healthy Minds*, 1.
3. Greenspan and Lewis, *Building Healthy Minds*.

4. Frank Tate, *Time Machines Work: Using the Pain from Your Past as Rocket Fuel for Your Future* (Concord, CA: 5 Minute Walk Management, Inc., 2020), 256–258.
5. Tate, *Time Machines Work*, 198–211.
6. Attachment researchers Kent Hoffman, Glen Cooper, and Bert Powell developed what's known as the Circle of Security, derived from the original research of British psychiatrist John Bowlby. For more information on how this works, visit Circle of Safety International at www.circleofsecurityinternational.com.
7. The connection between exploration, self-confidence, and self-competence is demonstrated in more than sixty studies on the topic. See the table of findings in Mikulincer and Shaver, *Attachment in Adulthood*, 155–160.
8. The principles of grace and truth and exploration and protection are explained in detail in *Safe House*, 70–109.
9. John Townsend, *Leadership Beyond Reason: How Great Leaders Succeed by Harnessing the Power of Their Values, Feelings, and Intuition* (Nashville: Thomas Nelson, 2009), 126.
10. Gottman and Gottman, *Emotion Coaching*.

14. DECISION 6: ESTABLISH FAMILY RHYTHMS

1. These insights come from J. Amanda McGuire, "Evening or Morning: When Does the Biblical Day Begin?," *Andrews University Seminary Studies* 46, no. 2 (Autumn 2008): 201–214, https://www.andrews.edu/library/car/cardigital/Periodicals/AUSS/2008/2008-2/2008-2-03.pdf.
2. To learn more about practicing a Shabbat meal, see Jefferson Bethke, *Take Back Your Family: From the Tyrants of Burnout, Busyness, Individualism, and the Nuclear Ideal* (Nashville: Thomas Nelson, 2021).
3. A huge thanks to Blake Smith and Jeremy Pryor for their insights in helping us nail down our family rhythm. Their insights from years of doing the same have saved us a ton of time.
4. Justin Whitmel Earley, *The Common Rule: Habits of Purpose for an Age of Distraction* (Downer's Grove, IL: InterVarsity Press, 2019).

15. DECISION 7: SET VALUES

1. "Value," *Merriam-Webster Dictionary*, https://www.merriam-webster.com/dictionary/value.
2. You can download the worksheet at www.famousathome.com/book.
3. As part of the discovery exercise, we also walk families through how they want to spend vacations and holidays and we help them create a bucket list. If you'd like to make this part of your discovery process, you can download the worksheet at www.famousathome.com/book.

4. You can download the worksheet at www.famousathome.com/book.

YOUR FAMILY MISSION

1. Timothy Keller, *The Freedom of Self-Forgetfulness: The Path to True Christian Joy* (Leyland, England: 10Publishing, 2012), 31–32.
2. Ronald Rolheiser, *Sacred Fire: A Vision for a Deeper Human and Christian Maturity* (New York: Crown Publishing Group, 2014), 309–310.
3. Rich Villodas (@richvillodas), Twitter, August 26, 2021, https://mobile.twitter.com/richvillodas/status/1431006735087570954.

ABOUT THE AUTHORS

Dr. Josh and Christi Straub are the cofounders of Famous at Home, an organization with the life-giving mission of cultivating connection, adventure, and purpose in families across the globe. Famous at Home is also a coaching organization that equips leaders, organizations, and churches in emotional intelligence and family wellness.

As speakers, authors, and marriage and leadership coaches, Josh and Christi host the weekly *Famous at Home* podcast and lead a yearlong coaching cohort called The Leader's Heart. They are the authors of three children's books: *What Am I Feeling?*, *What Do I Do with Worry?*, and *25 Days of the Christmas Story*. Josh is also the author of *Safe House: How Emotional Safety Is the Key to Raising Kids Who Live, Love, and Lead Well.*

Josh and Christi love spending time on the lake with their three sweet kids and their overly energetic goldendoodle, Copper.